TEACHING ENGLISH
in Secondary Schools

SAGE was founded in 1965 by Sara Miller McCune to support the dissemination of usable knowledge by publishing innovative and high-quality research and teaching content. Today, we publish more than 750 journals, including those of more than 300 learned societies, more than 800 new books per year, and a growing range of library products including archives, data, case studies, reports, conference highlights, and video. SAGE remains majority-owned by our founder, and after Sara's lifetime will become owned by a charitable trust that secures our continued independence.

Los Angeles | London | Washington DC | New Delhi | Singapore

TEACHING ENGLISH
in Secondary Schools
JOHN GORDON

Los Angeles | London | New Delhi
Singapore | Washington DC

Los Angeles | London | New Delhi
Singapore | Washington DC

SAGE Publications Ltd
1 Oliver's Yard
55 City Road
London EC1Y 1SP

SAGE Publications Inc.
2455 Teller Road
Thousand Oaks, California 91320

SAGE Publications India Pvt Ltd
B 1/I 1 Mohan Cooperative Industrial Area
Mathura Road
New Delhi 110 044

SAGE Publications Asia-Pacific Pte Ltd
3 Church Street
#10-04 Samsung Hub
Singapore 049483

Editor: James Clark
Assistant editor: Rachael Plant
Production editor: Tom Bedford
Copyeditor: Peter Williams
Proofreader: Caroline Stock
Indexer: John Gordon
Marketing manager: Dilhara Attygalle
Cover design: Naomi Robinson
Typeset by: C&M Digitals (P) Ltd, Chennai, India
Printed and bound by: CPI Group (UK) Ltd,
Croydon, CRO 4YY (for Antony Rowe)

MIX
Paper from
responsible sources
FSC
www.fsc.org   FSC® C013604

Library of Congress Control Number: 2014946914

British Library Cataloguing in Publication data

A catalogue record for this book is available from
the British Library

ISBN 978-1-4462-5316-8
ISBN 978-1-4462-5317-5 (pbk)

At SAGE we take sustainability seriously. Most of our products are printed in the UK using FSC papers and boards.
When we print overseas we ensure sustainable papers are used as measured by the Egmont grading system.
We undertake an annual audit to monitor our sustainability.

CONTENTS

About the author   vii
Acknowledgements   ix

Introduction: the knowledge of English teachers and this book   1

1 Lesson design for learning in English   15

2 Reading a set text   31

3 Analysing literary texts   44

4 Writing based on literary models   57

5 Teaching about language   73

6 Teaching points of grammar   86

7 Media and multiliteracies in English   101

8 Spoken language   118

9 Teaching Shakespeare   131

10 Teaching drama in English   145

11 Teaching poetry   160

12 Your growth as an English teacher   174

Index   187

ABOUT THE AUTHOR

Dr John Gordon is a lecturer and researcher in English Education at the University of East Anglia, a long-recognised provider of outstanding teacher education. He has led a successful Secondary PGCE(M) English course for fifteen years and has research interests in poetry education and pupils' responses to literature. Dr Gordon is the author of *A Pedagogy of Poetry – Through the Poems of W. B. Yeats* (Trentham/Institute of Education Press) and co-editor of *Preparing to Teach: Learning from Experience* (Routledge). He has published extensively in international journals such as *The Curriculum Journal, Changing English, English in Education, Educational Research* and *Classroom Discourse* and contributed chapters to *Poetry* and *Childhood* (Trentham) and *Making Poetry Matter: International Research on Poetry* (Bloomsbury).

ACKNOWLEDGEMENTS

Thanks to all the colleagues and students I meet in my role as a PGCE tutor. The book has been influenced by many conversations over fifteen years and is intended to reflect some of the issues in English teaching and learning that demand our attention during a course of teacher education. Students continue to work diligently and thoughtfully in a national context for training which is extremely demanding. Teachers and mentors support them with generosity and professionalism, and in doing so make a significant contribution to the future of the English discipline.

SAGE would like to thank the following people whose feedback on the original proposal helped to shape this book:

Anthony Archdeacon, Liverpool Hope University
Christopher Hanley, Manchester Metropolitan University
Karen Lockney, University of Cumbria
Vicky Macleroy, Goldsmiths, University of London
Annabel Watson, University of Exeter
John Yandell, Institute of Education, University of London

INTRODUCTION: THE KNOWLEDGE OF ENGLISH TEACHERS AND THIS BOOK

Objectives of this introduction:

- To explain the rationale of this book
- To present ways of looking at teachers' knowledge
- To explore what constitutes the distinctive knowledge of English teachers and how it relates to the organisation of chapters in this book
- To provide tools to trace and record your own developing knowledge for teaching English

This book aims to develop your thinking and judgement as an English teacher, and to help you understand ways of teaching in each of the major areas of English as set out in the National Curriculum. The chapters which follow build discussion around examples of lessons in English. In most cases, the book invites you to take on the role of observer and describes to you the progress of a lesson, the actions of a beginning teacher and the ways in which pupils respond. These illustrations are often followed by a report of discussion between the beginning teacher and their tutor or by extracts of the feedback the tutor provided for the student. This style aims to approximate what can be called knowledge-in-action, to convey the judgements that are made or could be made by a teacher in each situation.

It is important to say from the outset that this is not a book that sets out to guide you in techniques of classroom management. It also avoids suggesting that there is a 'right' way to teach aspects of English or a single approach relevant to each situation. The lessons described here are not ones in which student teachers encounter obvious problems of organisation or behaviour. In the majority of instances, pupils apparently make progress in learning. The discussion is interested in exploring the potential of an already sound basis for teaching, considering how small changes can allow different emphases, further engagement from pupils and, ideally, greater depth of learning. In this respect, then, the whole book is about deploying your knowledge as a teacher for optimum positive impact.

One significant challenge of beginning as a teacher is that you are always learning, though at each stage in your training your development will be linked to the Teachers' Standards. You will be expected to make progress. The tricky thing with English is that even though you may become more confident in, say, teaching around literary texts, for each new text you work with new subtleties will be relevant to the effect your teaching has on pupils' learning. However good your abilities in the last stages of your training, there will still be much to learn from how pupils respond to the topics and texts you are teaching for the first time. If you are alert to them your judgement is likely to improve. That is essential, because even when you are teaching a topic for the fifth time in your career, the class in front of you could react very differently to the previous four. Your experiences up to that point will give you a sense of the range of possible pupil responses, of the difficulties they may have and of a variety of strategies to use at different moments, whether with the whole class or to support individuals. The development of your teacherly knowledge is a process of constant review and refinement, and certainly not one where you eventually arrive at complete expertise or absolute mastery.

In the spirit of the English subject discipline, the descriptions of lessons found here are to some extent instances of creative writing. Each chapter is informed by the experiences of beginning teachers, by the sort of content they are asked to teach or create and by the dilemmas they face. Though actual lessons influence the examples, none of what you read here is a direct report of a lesson that really happened. Each instance is a composite or collage. Some aspects of these lessons have an origin in actual experience, but they are shaped to capture the generalisable issues that can arise for any beginning teacher of English. In this respect the teachers too are characters, with no connection to real individuals. The reported discussions and extracts from tutor feedback are based on typical exchanges, though none are verbatim transcriptions of dialogue that actually occurred.

I hope you find that this fictionalisation lends the book some validity and that by virtue of this form the book can ring true to your own experiences. After all, much of what we hope for in our teaching, as we plan lessons and anticipate classroom activity, happens in the imagination. We project a view of the lesson to come and create archetypes of what we believe a 'good' or 'outstanding' lesson to be. What you read here tries to avoid designating evaluative judgements like those but instead invites you to consider that any teaching, particularly your own teaching, could happen like this …
and this …
and this …

The knowledge you need to teach English well

When you learn to teach you will be aware of an area of competence often called 'subject knowledge'. Most programmes of teacher education here and abroad are organised according to professional standards, often defined by governments, and these usually include a section devoted to this category. The current Teachers' Standards for England are no exception, outlining a requirement that you 'demonstrate good subject and curriculum knowledge' (DfE, 2011: 11, item 3) in order to qualify. You will aim to meet the standard, but developing subject knowledge is not a simple process. Qualifying successfully does not mean that you arrive at a point where you complete the process of knowledge development, and you are unlikely to find an experienced teacher of English who feels they have reached an end to developing their understanding of the subject. Subject knowledge doesn't really work in absolutes, and your own feelings around it will shift as you train. On occasion you will feel very secure in your knowledge of a topic, enjoying leading a lesson about it and perhaps confident because you studied it in depth during your initial degree. At other times you will feel far less at ease, perhaps acutely conscious that though you can write complex sentences with flair, you will find it very hard to explain the difference between those and simple sentences to your Year 7 group. Even if you do feel secure with that example in terms of providing an explanation, it will not follow that you can guide your pupils through a process which allows them to understand and then use them effectively in their own writing. The example shows that you can know something yourself, but that knowing in this way is not quite the same as teaching it well.

The idea of subject knowledge in English is problematic. The National Curriculum frameworks for each key stage (DfE, 2013, 2014) indicate skills in grammar and vocabulary, reading, writing and spoken language that pupils should acquire as a result of your teaching, though the means for guiding them there are generally left to the discretion of the teacher. It is similar with the resources used in teaching, such as textbooks or online material: English teachers and their departments usually find they have some choice over which topics and texts they use. The content for teaching and learning in English does not have a consistently stable core, even in the domains everyone must teach. Take the study of Shakespeare, for example. Across the country, any number of his plays may be taught, and individual teachers will have varying familiarity with his canon. They won't share equivalent expertise or enthusiasm around the same plays, and each is likely to draw on different resources when they work around them. If there is necessary knowledge common to all, it revolves instead around *how* to teach Shakespeare plays, an awareness of approaches and techniques that can help pupils understand whichever play they are studying. Of course each teacher needs to know the study play well themselves, but how they apply that knowledge will also vary depending on the age of the class they are working with and the curricular context in which they work. The demands of a particular examination specification will influence their emphasis, but they will also need to consider the culture, interests and perspectives of the pupils they teach.

A model for describing the knowledge of an English teacher

It is very difficult to develop your knowledge as an English teacher if you are not quite sure what you are developing. There have been various attempts to describe the knowledge required of teachers generally, and they can be usefully applied to English teaching. Perhaps the most simple distinction to bear in mind is the difference between what you know yourself about a topic or text and knowing how to present it to other people, in this case pupils in the secondary age range.

You probably hold formal qualifications in areas of English and related subjects that are relevant to teaching English in secondary schools. It could be that you hold a degree in English Literature or Linguistics, or A-level qualifications in Theatre Studies or English Language. You are likely too to have acquired relevant knowledge through your leisure interests, probably as an enthusiastic reader (or viewer), as a writer or through involvement in drama productions. Think of what you know from these prior experiences as content, what you bring with you to your period of preparation as a teacher. You have a personal and unique archive of English-related experiences that constitute *content knowledge*.

The fact that you are working through a formal programme of teacher education suggests that the knowledge you have already is not in itself enough to equip you to teach. There must be some other sort of knowledge, a distinctly teacherly knowledge, that it is equally essential to acquire if you are to become a teacher. The earlier example of knowledge about Shakespeare shows that this could comprise knowledge of steps in teaching distinctive to each topic. The word 'pedagogy' means the craft or science of teaching and so the associated knowledge can be called *pedagogical knowledge*.

This distinction is apparent in a way of looking at teacher knowledge devised by the American educationalist Lee Shulman. Shulman has considered many forms of professional education beyond school teaching, including law and medicine, and so became interested in identifying principles that could apply across each form of professional preparation. In secondary phase education it is also useful that the model can be applied to very different subjects.

Shulman (1987) presented teacher knowledge organised into seven categories. The first, of *content knowledge*, we have already identified. Shulman divides our second category of *pedagogical knowledge* in two, seeing a distinction between the *general pedagogical knowledge* needed by all teachers (for example knowing how to structure a lesson or organise a group activity) and the *pedagogical content knowledge* specific to their discipline. He defined the latter as 'that special amalgam of content and pedagogy that is uniquely the province of teachers, their own special form of professional understanding' (1987: 64). As you begin to teach you will encounter this as the special combination of your own knowledge about texts and topics and what you learn about processes of teaching through your experience in the English classroom. You will see and use processes and methods unique to your subject, and also unique to topics within the subject. What steps are sensible to work through when teaching pupils about metaphor, for example?

The other four categories Shulman proposes are these:

- knowledge of the curriculum;
- knowledge of learners and their characteristics;
- knowledge of educational contexts; and
- knowledge of educational ends, purposes and values.

Even if we accept Shulman's categories, the relationship between them in practice is hard to pin down. One of his own remarks about English gives us a clue as to why this might be so:

> The teacher of English should know English and American prose and poetry, written and spoken language use and comprehension and grammar ... with the critical literature that applies to particular novels or epics ... [and] understand alternative theories of interpretation and criticism and *how these might relate to the issues of curriculum and teaching*. (Shulman, 1987: 65 [my italics])

The statement might seem reasonable, but if you try to work to this description as you learn to teach you will soon run into difficulty. When there is so much prose and poetry from each country, how do you decide which texts you must know if it is not possible to know them all? Does knowing them simply mean that you have read novels, poems and short stories, and seen plays? The same dilemma of selection applies to theories and critics: which ones? In language work, should your practice be informed by any particular theoretical models? English is used differently between England and the United States. In whichever of the two you work, or whether you are based somewhere else entirely, which standard form should you adopt and what should be your attitude to non-standard uses of the language?

Though it is appealing to formulate a list of things you should know and do, most English teaching is difficult to capture in checklists. While you can set about reading *The Tempest* if you are going to teach it, the fact that you have read it won't prove that you have good *pedagogical content knowledge* around it. Teaching it successfully demands that you understand its distinctive challenges and how to help pupils respond as thoroughly and deeply as possible. One unique dimension of teaching the play could concern helping pupils understand how Ariel ~~~~liban reflect facets of Prospero's personality or, further, human way you approach this won't apply to how you teach any of e's other plays, though there will be some common ground around characterisation and symbolism that could be partially replicated in teaching other literary works.

However subtle your grasp of relevant *pedagogical content knowledge*, it alone won't help you teach well. Your professional work in the classroom and across the school will demand the interplay of different categories of knowledge at different times. Your knowledge of learners will be crucial both in terms of what you understand of the psychology of learning and maturation through adolescence, as will your knowledge of your pupils as individuals. You will need to know about the English curriculum, whether the National Curriculum or one devised by your school, and this will to some extent define the necessary *pedagogical content knowledge* and *subject content knowledge* too. You may need to be less active in furthering your knowledge of the *educational context*, as you will have first-hand knowledge of your institution, but there may be scope to consider the nature of the local community and the contexts in which pupils live, work and play outside the school. It is also useful to acknowledge and articulate what you see as the ends, purposes and values of education and to be very conscious of the degree to which these align with those of your school, those of the curriculum and those of society in general. Whether implicit or declared, these will shape an ethos that will influence your teaching. In the long term being aware of these aspects could help you adapt to varying circumstances in the different schools you work in across your career, and support your journey to whatever type of teacher you aspire to be. During your teaching from one day to the next your thinking and practice across these areas will require discernment and judgement, what one commentator terms 'complex responsiveness' (Nussbaum, 1990: 55) to the demands of your immediate situation, whatever the restrictions or opportunities it presents in any given moment.

You may be familiar with John Dewey as the originator of a library classification system. In that achievement he devised a system for the organisation of knowledge in the form of books, but he also considered the nature of knowledge in less material form. He was especially interested in the link between thinking and action, and was pioneering in exploring the development of teachers' knowledge and how to become more 'knowing' in your chosen profession through your continued practice of it. For Dewey (1904), *intelligent action* as you learn your craft means going beyond observing and imitating experienced colleagues to exercise judgement. This can be informed by what you know of the content for teaching (that is, *content knowledge*) but also what you notice and consider of the process of learning. The judgements you make put knowledge into action (Dewey called it knowledge-in-action). In his time as Secretary of State for Education, Michael Gove asserted that 'watching others and being rigorously observed yourself as you develop is the best route to acquiring mastery in the classroom' (Gove, 2010). While many in the profession – indeed most – would agree that observation is an important part of the process of learning to teach, Dewey indicates that it is not the only dimension. It entails something more active, and actively thoughtful, if your actions in the classroom are to develop and refine. You only have to reflect on the nature of English, having much of its substance in reading and writing activity, to recognise that it must in very great part attend to private processes of thought and their development in pupils, and so complementary thought by teachers is likely to be as significant as what is visible in public, shared activity in the subject. One study (Ethel and McMeniman, 2000) tried to find out how beginning teachers unlock the *knowledge-in-action* of more experienced expert colleagues. The study looked at working relationship between a beginning teacher and their mentor, and the importance of dialogue between the two which makes explicit and gives access to 'the thinking underlying expert teaching' (2000: 99). They argued that mentoring conversations have the capacity to support students' 'understanding of the relationships between the theoretical and practical components' (2000: 98) of learning to teach. In effect, these conversations are likely to discuss the interplay of the various categories of knowledge outlined by Shulman, even though participants may not be aware of the labels he gives them.

Some studies of teacher knowledge look at it as something that exists not only in individuals but collectively too. In school, this is apparent in the sort of communal understanding shared by a subject department or faculty. Viv Ellis (2007), for example, described *collective knowledge* where members of a department community build and shape a shared understanding of what the role of English teacher entails and the knowledge it requires (their own *practice*) in relation to the wider *culture* of the subject created through government policies, curricular details, the history of the discipline and examination requirements.

A system for capturing your teacherly knowledge

In many training courses it is a requirement to record your subject knowledge development, often in some sort of written document or online portfolio. The course I lead uses two complementary mechanisms. They aim to support the subject knowledge development of each beginning teacher as a log of what they know and come to know during training, also identifying the next steps needed to extend or deepen knowledge.

One item is called the Subject Knowledge Record (see Figure 1). Its format uses Shulman's ideas of *content knowledge* and *pedagogical content knowledge*, matching them with the curricular framework that students work with most frequently in their daily teaching – in this case the latest version of the National Curriculum (DfE, 2013, 2014). Students first record details on the format in the opening three weeks of training at the university, after discussion with their tutor. Once students begin placement in school, they discuss the record with their mentor. The mentor seeks to balance opportunities for the students to teach in areas of secure content knowledge with areas that the record suggests are less familiar. Over the full programme the record supports the planning of opportunities that allow students some experience of the breadth of the curriculum. In practice, that means having first-hand experience teaching as many curriculum topics as possible. Additional methods of ensuring a broad knowledge include marking samples of pupils' work to understand how assessment works relative to curricular detail, or observing teaching colleagues presenting topics that may be unfamiliar to you. The rationale is explained for students in the hand-book as follows:

We hold the position that subject knowledge is not finite and that there is never a point where you know everything there is to know. However, you are expected to acquire knowledge of the breadth of the curriculum during training, and demonstrate certain dispositions to this development. Accordingly, the purpose of the record is primarily formative, the information you add to it indicative of your developing expertise. As such, it also serves as a diagnostic device for mentors and tutors to guide you.

Specifically it is intended to:

- acknowledge the experience you arrive with;
- support all staff involved in your training in understanding the breadth of your experience across placements;
- guide the range of experience – ideally to be as broad as possible during your training and certainly for you to have some experience linked with each heading of the curriculum.

Curricular Knowledge strand	Content Knowledge (CK)	Pedagogic Content Knowledge (PCK)
Writing	Record details of relevant study (A-level, uni modules …), experience (teaching roles, other professional roles …) and texts/topics encountered during training.	This section details strategies and approaches relevant to this area of the curriculum.
Write accurately, fluently, effectively and at length for pleasure and information through: *writing for a wide range of purposes and audiences, including:* • well-structured formal expository and narrative essays	Planning, drafting and organising academic essays. Proofreading. Referencing. Writing for a range of purposes/audiences: • narrative essays • persuasive writing • creative writing • formal dissertation	☐ supporting pupils in establishing purposes and genres for writing ☐ guiding pupils about the conventions of specific forms, including rhetorical and literary devices ☐ providing apt and stimulating model texts as examples
• stories, scripts, poetry and other imaginative writing • notes and polished scripts for talks and presentations • a range of other narrative and non-narrative texts, including arguments, personal and formal letters • summarising and organising material, and supporting ideas and arguments with any necessary factual detail • applying their growing knowledge of vocabulary, grammar and text structure to their writing and selecting the appropriate form • drawing on knowledge of literary and rhetorical devices from their reading and listening to enhance the impact of their writing.	English teacher education sessions at university covering processes of composition and review across Key Stages 3 and 4. Knowledge of vocabulary/grammar through experience of discrete grammar teaching. Degree in English Literature – experienced in literary analysis and use of related terminology.	☐ guiding and modelling approaches to note-making ☐ presenting writing frames where appropriate, with appropriate flexibility ☐ guide pupils towards cohesion in texts ☐ explain, model and guide paragraph use **Opportunity to teach writing for a variety of forms and purposes** ☐ narrative prose ☐ descriptive prose ☐ poetry ☐ drama scripts ☐ non-fiction forms (add details) **Writing with electronic media** ☐ IT – word processor, email, blog, etc. Assess fictional / creative forms ☐ KS3 ☐ KS4 **Assess non-fiction forms ☐ KS3 ☐ KS4** ☐ respond to ideas and voice in marking ☐ attend to sentence structure and punctuation in marking

Figure 1 Extract of a Subject Knowledge Record, mapping curricular knowledge against notes on content knowledge and developing pedagogical content knowledge

The handbook asks that students 'avoid mere coverage', explaining that the items should be used to prompt discussion with English colleagues about what constitutes rich pupil experience or excellent teaching in each area. If you look at the current Teachers' Standards you will see that one of the descriptors of outstanding attainment during training (DfE, 2011: 11, item 4, 'Plan and teach well-structured, lessons') describes the key ability to 'reflect systematically on the effectiveness of lessons and approaches to teaching'. Another item emphasises your wider professional responsibility 'for improving teaching through appropriate professional development, responding to advice and feedback from colleagues' (2011: 13, item 8) and hence using your initiative to make and explore opportunities for doing so. Each of these links with the standard requiring you to 'demonstrate good subject and curriculum knowledge' (2011: 11, item 3), which encompasses having secure knowledge in your specialism, using that knowledge to maintain 'pupils' interest in the subject', and your capacity to address any misunderstandings exhibited by pupils. At the same time you are expected to 'demonstrate a critical understanding of developments in the subject and curriculum areas, and promote the value of scholarship'.

A second item used in the course is the Subject Knowledge Journal. Students complete journal entries at four points in their training, responding to questions they choose from a list of several. In our programme we ask that journal entries are made on two occasions during each placement. To use the questions yourself, choose a domain of English in which you are working with your pupils, such as reading non-fiction, or vocabulary enrichment to support descriptive writing. You can respond to whichever questions are most relevant to your experience. If you opt to write a response, keep it brief: between 250 and 500 words is the guide range.

(a) What aspects in this domain of English are new or unfamiliar to you?
(b) What is the relationship between your existing *content knowledge* (what you know already from your studies) and the *pedagogical content knowledge* you are developing through teaching (knowing about ways to teach the topic or text)? Where do the two types of knowledge overlap? Where do you find gaps and new things you need to know?
(c) As you teach your pupils, what have you found out about their difficulties or misconceptions in this domain of English?
(d) What do you think is the most important thing you have learnt about conceptualising this domain of English for presentation to pupils?

(Continued)

(Continued)

(e) Are there details of your knowledge and experience that you find difficult to link with curriculum details? If so, what is the source of that difficulty?

(f) What bearing does the context for assessment (for example examination requirements) have in defining the *content knowledge* pupils need in this area? What does it emphasise or exclude?

(g) Can you articulate your underlying aims and purposes in this area?

(h) What aspects of *pedagogical content knowledge* have you recognised you have to develop in this domain?

The questions are devised to highlight the difference between teacherly knowledge (*pedagogical content knowledge*) and the knowledge you bring from earlier studies (i.e. *content knowledge*). Your learning in the area of *pedagogical content knowledge* will be dependent on your practical experience of teaching but also on your capacity to reflect on that and to identify ways to present and organise topics in English successfully to help pupils.

Questions (a) and (b) consider the distinctiveness of knowledge used in the classroom. For example, you may feel you have secure *subject content knowledge* around the concepts of accent and dialect. During teaching, however, you may find that your knowledge of pupils' local language use is limited (a) and also see that articulating the distinction between accent and dialect is as important as defining the terms discretely (b).

Questions (c) and (d) require your reflection about how pupils think about and come to understand the immediate topic, and then how recognising this can inform your own judgement as a teacher. For instance, if you find that pupils tend to muddle the distinction between accent and dialect (they commonly conflate the two), you would probably think very carefully about how you define them, how you emphasise the difference and explain it, what examples to use and the sequence in which you introduce both terms.

Questions (e) and (f) prompt thinking about what you already know yourself and how it is presented in the official curriculum or in the bespoke curriculum devised by your school. Sometimes you will encounter confusing differences in terminology, for instance where the grammar term 'conjunction' (see DfE, 2013: 10) may subsumed in the plural noun 'connectives' (a term introduced as part of the National Literary Strategy at the turn of the millennium, with a potent legacy!). The questions hint at the arbitrary curricularisation of knowledge, where information can be framed differently from its original conception in academia, or where the emphases of assessments shape presentation of content in unique ways.

Question (g) asks you to look beyond the content and reflect on what you are teaching it for: what is your pedagogical motivation for presenting this topic? What outcomes do you seek and how do they link to what you believe English to be for? Question (h) encourages an evaluative approach, and may lead you to develop an informal mental map or taxonomy of the curriculum domain you are working in. Doing so can help you see what makes up the domain with regard to terminology, concepts, processes, key resources and pupils' misconceptions, and can help you see around which aspects you still need to develop knowledge and understanding.

As you complete journal entries like this you are bound to reflect according to Shulman's categories of *subject content knowledge* and *pedagogical content knowledge*. At the same time, it is almost impossible to comment without also drawing on your knowledge of learners, of the context for learning or on what you know of curricular detail. Even where you are not responding directly to the question about values and purposes, it is probable that you will express these overtly or reveal them tacitly in your discussion. Furthermore, the design makes it possible to consider how the various types of knowledge work together in varying combinations. It allows any reader some insight into how you think as a teacher, which otherwise can only be inferred through your visible practice. It also gives you a record over time. No doubt you will see your own quality of reflection developing as well as the knowledge your entries describe.

References

Dewey, John (1904) 'The relation of theory to practice in education', in R. Archambault (ed.) (1974), *John Dewey on Education: Selected Writings*. Chicago: University of Chicago Press.

DfE (2011) *Teachers' Standards*. Reference: DFE-00066-2011.

DfE (2013) *English Programmes of Study: Key Stage 3 (National Curriculum in England)*. Reference: DFE-00184-2013.

DfE (2014) *English Programmes of Study: Key Stage 4 (National Curriculum in England)*. Reference: DFE-00497-2014.

Ellis, Viv (2007) 'Taking subject knowledge seriously: from professional knowledge recipes to complex conceptualizations of teacher development', *Curriculum Journal*, 18 (4): 447–62.

Ethel, Ruth G. and McMeniman, Marilyn M. (2000) 'Unlocking the knowledge in action of an expert practitioner', *Journal of Teacher Education*, 51: 87–101.

Gove, Michael (2010) Speech to the National College annual conference. Online at: http://www.michaelgove.com/content/national_college_annual_conference. (accessed 2 February 2012)

Nussbaum, Martha C. (1990) *Love's Knowledge: Essays On Philosophy and Literature*. Oxford: Oxford University Press.

Shulman, Lee S. (1987) 'Knowledge and teaching: foundations of the new reform', in J. Leach and B. Moon (eds), *Learners and Pedagogy*. Milton Keynes: Open University Press, pp. 61–77.

CHAPTER 1

LESSON DESIGN FOR LEARNING IN ENGLISH

Objectives of this chapter:

- To consider the thought process behind lesson preparation
- To present a distinction between lesson planning and lesson design
- To assist you in developing challenging and precise learning objectives
- To help you understand how precise objectives relate to lesson activities and pupils' progress in learning

---

Introduction

This chapter has a relationship with everything that follows in this book. It is about designing lessons and preparation for teaching. It looks at the skills you need to put together lessons in which pupils learn and make progress in English, and at the related thinking and decision-making that contributes to success in the classroom. The phrase 'lesson design' is used very deliberately as an alternative to 'lesson planning'. The latter phrase, the more commonly used, suggests a schedule of activities that you work through with a class during a lesson. While deciding on a sensible sequence of engaging activity is an important dimension of preparing for teaching, a focus on these aspects alone doesn't quite capture everything that you do. Somewhere in your deliberation you may have in mind an ethos for your teaching, some guiding values and principles that may be tacit in your eventual lesson content. There will also be aspects of presentation to consider where aesthetic choices have some influence on pupils' learning, for instance in how you design a supporting worksheet, or the arrangement of PowerPoint slides. The nature of the school timetable framing your work will have an impact on the rhythm of your teaching: some of you will work in schools where 45-minute lessons impel urgency, some of you will work in 60-minute sessions, and others will teach lessons of around 90 minutes duration which could afford different opportunities for combining two or more phases affording depth of engagement.

Not one of these items is specific to English or the pupils you teach. You will also have to take care in establishing what dimension of English merits emphasis in the immediate lesson and must often take additional responsibility for selecting the material suited to your aim. It sounds more straightforward than it is. In almost any subject in the curriculum pupils are asked to read, write, speak and listen during lessons. Clearly this is true of English, presenting teachers of the subject with opportunities and a very specific dilemma. On one hand, it means you can find connections between those different skills that have potential to be rich and enjoyable for pupils. On the other, your success as a teacher in supporting pupils' progress can often depend on how precise you are in identifying the particular skills you want pupils to develop in the lesson being prepared. Given that pupils will use many and diverse language skills in each English lesson, isolating and emphasising the most relevant ones can be challenging. The problem is most obvious in literary study. The emphasis is usually on pupils' responses to text and thus developing their reading skills. However, these skills are often demonstrated through writing, for example in formal assignments or creative pieces written from the perspective of a central character. The skills pupils need to write in either of these forms are very different from one another, and different too from the reading skills the pieces are intended to capture.

Finally, your design of lessons responds to the pupils that you work with on a weekly basis, having their own interests and enthusiasms as individuals and with their unique dynamics collectively in class groups. You will introduce items in one way rather than another because you know it will particularly help one pupil to grasp the topic, or use an analogy because you realise it resonates with what you know most of a class watch on TV, with the music they listen to or the sports that interest them. Some of this will happen spontaneously during teaching, but often it will be strategic too, resulting from choice, an element in a design. And the way you shape your lessons, including the space you give pupils for independent work, will reflect your concept of 'a pupil' – what they can do, the boundaries within which they work and the nature of their relationship with their teacher and with the subject.

The influence of the curriculum on lesson design

The information you draw on to decide what to teach will vary depending on the department you are working in, the age and level of the class and where you are in the stages of your teacher education. If you are in a first placement in the first term of your training course, you could find yourself devising lessons one at a time, probably with the guidance of a mentor or the usual class teacher. They might indicate to you the precise content and skills each lesson needs to address. In other situations, you will have access to contextual information and more responsibility and choice for deciding what pupils need to learn and how to approach it. This supporting information is likely to be in the form of a 'scheme of work', an overview for teaching the topic in hand, signalling the expected outcomes, activities and assessments that typically comprise this unit and often archived with supporting resources too. In some departments you may be given work booklets, worksheets and PowerPoint presentations that you are expected to incorporate into your own lessons.

The information provided by your department is likely to be connected to the most recent version of the National Curriculum (Key Stage 3: DfE, 2013; Key Stage 4: DfE, 2014a), though since its publication some schools have had greater freedom in their relationship with this according to their status. Academies and free schools are not obliged to follow it but instead have scope to devise their own curriculum for English as they do for other subjects. In schools that belong to a chain (a group of academy schools connected either locally or nationally) you may find the English department working to a curriculum shared by the whole group. Some organisations have appointed curriculum advisors with the role of designing and implementing their bespoke curriculum across each school in the chain.

Each curricular framework, whether the National Curriculum or an in-house system, will indicate the skills pupils are expected to develop in English and the content to be addressed. In English this often entails stipulating the experience pupils should have with respect to language use, knowledge of grammar, and literary texts and approaches to them.

We will use the National Curriculum as the example framework in this chapter and throughout the book, concentrating on the skills you need to interpret and use a curricular framework so that the principles can be applied to those alternative arrangements too. Wherever you teach, you will find that as well as taking into account a curriculum, you will also need to be aware of the linked assessment framework. At Key Stage 3, between the ages of 11 and 14, this is very flexible, and all schools have the scope to assess as they see fit, providing the system works in the interests of their pupils and supports their progress in learning:

> Assessment levels have now been removed and will not be replaced. Schools have the freedom to develop their own means of assessing pupils' progress towards end of key stage expectations. (DfE, 2014b: 3)

At Key Stage 4, covering ages 14 to 16, assessment practice tends to be directed by the formal examination system, with English departments looking to the detail of GCSE specifications for guidance. The process of curriculum reform reflected this in simultaneous publication of new curricular details for Key Stage 4 and revised specifications for English and English Literature at GCSE. Specifications can derive from any one of the major examination boards relevant to England, Wales or Northern Ireland. The Ofqual website provides an up-to-date overview of participating examination boards at any given time.

Deciding what to teach in your lesson

When you come to the point of designing a lesson, you are likely to have to formulate objectives. These are usually termed 'learning objectives' so that emphasis falls on the development you intend to support in your pupils. These may be provided for you in your department's scheme of work or you may need to devise them yourself to express development that has some link with the curriculum framework relevant to your setting. Wherever you teach, they can often be phrased in terms of knowledge, skills and understanding.

Lesson design: an example

Arthur has prepared a lesson around *Romeo and Juliet*, focused on the first act which communicates to the audience information about the protagonists as each one speaks with friends or family members. In Act 1, scene 1, Romeo speaks to Benvolio about Juliet, while in Act 1, scene 3 Juliet, the Nurse and Lady Capulet debate Juliet's marriage to Paris.

Learning objective: To understand how Shakespeare presents the characters to us in this scene.		
Phase	Duration	Activity
1	5 mins	Introduce objective, give context for this scene and recap previous reading
2	10 mins	Pupils read the exchange between Romeo and Benvolio – individual reading
3	5 mins	Plenary recap – establishing what happened in this extract
4	10 mins	Questions about the scene: pupils copy down the quotations and answer the questions linked to each
5	10 mins	Pupils read the exchange between Juliet, Nurse and Lady Capulet – individual reading
6	5mins	Plenary recap – establishing what happened in this extract
7	10 mins	Questions about the scene: pupils copy down the quotations and answer the questions linked to each
8	5 mins	Set homework

Figure 1.1 Arthur's *Romeo and Juliet* lesson plan

On paper, Arthur's preparation is very much a plan in the sense of a schedule rather than a design (see Figure 1.1). It starts with an objective Arthur has devised himself, linked with the department's Year 8 scheme of work on Shakespeare, 'to understand how Shakespeare presents the characters to us in this scene'. When Arthur taught the lesson, it went smoothly insofar as pupils worked through the listed activities. They were compliant with Arthur's instructions and in that respect things very literally went to plan. Even before teaching, however, it is possible to look at Arthur's lesson details and anticipate its limited impact on pupils' learning in terms of the stated objectives. It does not offer a coherent design because it does not describe activities or even phases to match the learning objective. The questions Arthur asks of his pupils direct them to significant details in each scene, and even to relevant information that suggests something of each character's feelings, but no part of his plan signals that time will be spent addressing the *presentation* of the characters. His tutor remarked:

> The objective you shared with pupils has links with the textual detail considered today but you did not address it in a way that would help pupils make progress in their understanding of *presentation* specifically. This aspect deserves more focused attention in your lesson design and more emphasis during teaching if you are sure this is what you want pupils to learn about. However, it is possible given your lesson content and the questions you ask that you are actually more interested in *comprehension* than Shakespeare's presentation. In that case you need to reshape your objectives so they are about making sense of the scene rather than analysing Shakespeare's craft.

The steps in Arthur's plan attend more to exploring the psychology of characters, tacitly accepting them as real people whose motives and thoughts we might explain. This is useful activity, but not what Arthur has set out to teach according to his stated objectives. You will notice too that Arthur's lesson has a repetitive structure, with the phases of reading and questioning repeated. This may have benefit in that pupils get used to an approach to the text in the first part of the lesson and then consolidate it in the second half. However, because the tasks don't match Arthur's learning objective and because the questions make similar demands of pupils in each phase, the plan in this form does not convey how pupils will make progress in learning.

Redesigning Arthur's lesson

Arthur can improve the likely impact of his teaching with a different conception of preparation, thinking more in terms of design and less in terms of a schedule. He needs to look again at his learning objective, though it is understandable that he phrases it in general terms if he looks to the National Curriculum 'subject content' details for Reading (DfE, 2013: 4) as a model. Its details about reading 'critically' give a context for a lesson focused on presentation in this statement, 'knowing how language, including figurative language, vocabulary choice, grammar, text structure and organisational features present meaning'. Conversely, if Arthur wants to encompass dramatic elements, these details are more relevant: 'understanding how the work of dramatists is communicated effectively through performance and how alternative staging allows for different interpretations of a play'. Other emphases, including characterisation, are signalled in 'studying setting, plot, and characterisation, and the effects of these'.

It is not surprising to find that these are generalised references as the curriculum statements apply to the full range of literary texts prescribed for study at Key Stage 3. In this form, however, they don't really support Arthur in finding adequate focus for what he wants pupils to learn in relation to this extract during this lesson. Arthur needs to draw on these prompts from the curriculum but to break them down further into components relevant to the knowledge, understanding and skills that he wants pupils to develop. The success of a lesson can depend on the teacher's ability to express clearly and precisely the learning objectives at the design stage. Often you will wish to communicate these to the class directly during teaching as well. Because they provide for pupils the most overt expression of the point of their activity, it is essential that they are well-formulated. Arthur also needs to consider the lesson structure, so that it too affords progress in pupils' learning. Clear objectives can point towards the necessary steps.

Arthur can find greater clarity by identifying the new knowledge to be introduced and retained by pupils in the lesson. We can think of this as the knowledge content, as information that might be transmitted by explanation or statement. In the study of a scene from Shakespeare, this might include basic knowledge of a character's actions (for instance knowing that Juliet disobeys her father), or identifying a change in their emotions from one point of the act to another (for instance the contrast we see in Juliet, antagonistic to her mother in scene 3, tender with Romeo in scene 5). Your own expertise as a teacher should help you recognise the sort of details that pupils need to know or hold on to in order to understand the immediate extract for study and its place in the whole play.

It is also useful to make a distinction between this sort of knowledge, which might be introduced through statements and assimilated through repetition and rote learning, and more sophisticated understanding. In a scene drawn from *Romeo and Juliet*, you may want pupils to consider why Romeo acts as he does or in another extract to develop empathy with Juliet. These outcomes require a different sort of engagement with the play, the first needing some appreciation of motive and causality and the second some capacity to identify with Juliet's circumstances and to appreciate events from her point of view. Though a pupil could be given a statement about Romeo's actions or Juliet's feelings, to understand those things in context is different from knowing they are relevant.

A third component to include in objectives concerns the skills you want pupils to acquire, consolidate or develop. As an English teacher you receive most of your information about pupils' knowledge and understanding through their verbal expression, whether written or oral. The skills they use to express ideas in each mode are paralleled by the programmes of study in the English National Curriculum, so that capacity relevant to Reading will often be apparent as pupils use skills framed in either the Writing or Spoken Language programmes of study (for each see DfE, 2013). Recent changes to the assessment framework, especially at GCSE where end-of-course examinations dominate (Ofqual, 2013: 5), mean that pupils' skills in writing will influence the outcomes of assessments of reading. In our Shakespeare example, Arthur needs to give careful thought to how he wants his pupils to express their developing capacity to read a Shakespeare play. If he really does want to focus on *presentation* as his original objective indicates, he needs to specify a related skill, for instance: 'to be able to explain in writing how figurative language helps us understand characters' feelings'. If he decides his lesson is less about presentation and more about establishing steps in the development of *characterisation*, a relevant skill might be for pupils 'to summarise orally how Romeo changes between the start and end of the scene'.

Formulating coherent learning objectives

We can formulate two sets of objectives for each path open to Arthur on the basis of his initial plan. If he wants pupils to learn about presentation, he might frame objectives like this:

- Know that Shakespeare uses dialogue to present information about Romeo and Juliet.
- Understand how the dialogue of characters presents their differing opinions about the relationship between Romeo and Juliet.
- Skills: be able to explain in writing how at least two different opinions about the relationship are presented through dialogue.

Note how the formulation of these objectives remains coherent, with the idea of *presentation* unifying the items. The same principle can be demonstrated in a separate set of objectives, which this time are focused more on character and are therefore more consistent with what Arthur actually included in his lesson:

- Know that Romeo and Juliet both feel strongly that they should see each other but that their friends and family do not always agree.
- Understand why their friends and family do not agree.
- Skills: to identify in the scene quotations that demonstrate the different opinions and to paraphrase them verbally.

This group of objectives coheres around the idea of differing opinions too, but it does not suggest that Arthur wants his pupils to remark on the details in the text with associated attention to Shakespeare's craft as a playwright. The first group is more interested in teaching about dialogue as a presentational device whereas these are concerned with appreciating the varying perspectives evident in the scene. If Arthur wants to introduce the key idea for either lesson it is now easier for him to do so, and in such a way that the distinction between the two options would be clear to pupils. In one lesson he would be teaching 'how Shakespeare uses dialogue to present different opinions' and in the other it would be 'understanding different views about Romeo and Juliet's relationship'.

In terms of your own lesson design, it can help to ask these questions:

- Am I clear in my own mind about the 'key idea' or crux of the lesson?
- Can I articulate the key idea to pupils in simple terms?
- Am I clear about the lesson's learning objectives (knowledge, skills and understanding)?
- How will these objectives be communicated clearly to pupils?

Once Arthur formulates objectives along the lines suggested above, it will be easier for him to design the lesson so that there is logical progression through phases and for each phase to have a clear purpose in relation to the objectives which can also be shared with pupils. During the lesson, it will be easier for Arthur to make the links between phases because in one version of the lesson he can emphasise the role of dialogue at each stage and in the other he will stress the differing opinions.

Finding a structure for your lesson

Once Arthur formulates clear objectives he can begin to design the lesson's structure. He can start with questions like these, which begin with how the lesson content relates to the objectives:

- What steps are necessary to achieve the learning objectives?
- How should the steps be sequenced?
- How can I vary activity to sustain pupils' interest and motivation?
- What resources are necessary, and when and how should I introduce them?
- Is the development of the lesson practical to manage?

The rationale for his sequence can be informed by the work of Robert Gagné and Jerome Bruner, both of whom paid attention to sequences of learning in their studies.

Bruner (1966) developed ideas which are now widely discussed in terms of 'scaffolding', which means teaching designed with supports to assist pupils' progress. Robert Gagné (1970: 285) extended this thinking by describing lessons as a series of 'instructional events'. He argued that any unit of learning constitutes eight events, each with a clear and discrete purpose. The purpose of each event is as follows:

1. To activate the learner's motivation.
2. To inform the learner of the learning objectives.
3. To direct the attention of the learner.
4. To stimulate the learner to recall their relevant prior learning.
5. To provide the learner with guidance for their learning activity, whether a process, exercise or activity.
6. To enhance the capacity of the learner to retain the knowledge, skills or understanding developed in the fifth event.
7. To promote the learner's ability to transfer what has been learnt to other situations and contexts.
8. To elicit the performance of the learner in the process, exercise or activity and provide the learner with feedback about their performance.

Arthur's original lesson had stages to mirror most of these purposes, and even the repetition in that initial structure could be said to correspond to the sixth and seventh purposes here given that pupils would transfer the same manner of response to a second set of questions. One omission from the first plan concerns Gagné's final item, which aims to assess pupils' progress relative to step 2, the introduction of objectives. Here we can begin to see how complex lesson design is and the interdependence of each element. Because Arthur's original lesson objective lacked specificity, it would prove very difficult for him to gauge pupils' progress relative to it even if the activities had a more direct link. He doesn't include any mechanism by which pupils can show their understanding of presentation, and (even if he does include a phase to match the eighth purpose) there is no definition or explanation of modes of presentation for pupils in the early phases of the lesson. Without those sorts of clear explanations as a touchstone, the lesson design makes it very difficult for Arthur to gauge the extent to which pupils have assimilated the knowledge, still less how far they have understood it.

By contrast, if Arthur can be more precise as we have demonstrated in the newly phrased objectives, it is easier for him to gauge pupils' learning because recognition of how this information becomes available to him is inherent in the skills objectives. In one version he will know how well they understand the role of dialogue through what they write, and in the other he will hear how well they understand the different viewpoints through their verbal summaries articulated in their own words. By identifying the skills pupils must develop, Arthur's revised objectives concurrently indicate the mode of assessment, the means by which Arthur will know the extent of pupils' learning.

From objectives and sequence to activity design

Learning objectives state the knowledge, skills and understanding pupils will develop. They do not state what the teacher or pupils will *do* to make progress. There is at this stage no reference to the activities that constitute the vehicle for learning according to these. Arthur could draw from the repertoire of common arrangements used in English classrooms, such as paired discussion, individual response to a worksheet, answering questions posed in a textbook, role play, cloze exercises or annotation of the play. The objectives themselves suggest a movement from acquisition of knowledge, through assimilation which supports understanding, to skill development facilitating expression of a particular aspect of learning. Having the clarity of focus drawn from single, precisely identified concepts can contribute to a sense of rigour and purpose in your lessons. Ultimately, you may be teaching lessons to pupils of varying ages or abilities that actually have as their foundation the same objectives. The features most likely to differ, however, are the timescale (where you might cover three objectives in one lesson with one group, it could take three lessons with another), the activities you choose as the means of teaching them, and the levels of skill and understanding you expect. The access you provide for pupils to different levels of understanding will relate to the differentiation of your lessons, and overlaps with Bruner's idea of scaffolding (Bruner, 1966).

   Arthur is studying a literary text with his class, so one of his first decisions is about which part of the text to use as the basis of the lesson. We can see in the original plan his choice, so he then has to consider how he wants to introduce the extract, how it should be presented (on the page, read aloud, through film or acted out?) and what pupils need to do in response. This decision will lead him in turn to others about resourcing, for instance about whether to prepare questions or prompts, to provide written scaffolds in print or to project details for the class through a PowerPoint or Prezi presentation. Whatever choices he makes here, he also needs to reflect on how and when resources will be shared, whether the same resources will be used by all pupils, or if they will have a choice. Further, Arthur must decide how he will allocate lesson time to each activity, judging what is necessary in terms of pupils' engagement and what is appropriate relative to the emphasis of the learning objectives.

Designing mechanisms for gauging pupils' progress in learning

Parallel to thinking about the activities pupils must complete, Arthur should give some thought to how he will know they are making progress in learning. In doing so, his preparation links with the Teaching Standard relevant to planning and teaching (DfE, 2011: 11, item 4) and to the item focused on 'promoting good progress and outcomes by pupils' (DfE, 2011: 10, item 2). As Gagné's model (1970) indicates, the teacher can gauge progress at the end of the lesson in a plenary phase, but if Arthur designs other activities carefully he can learn something about whether the knowledge and understanding he hopes pupils will develop are reasonably secure before asking them to link them to a new skill. Though he will not have a major piece of work to draw on, he can find out about progress throughout the lesson by means of observation, swift questioning and listening. He could decide to build in interim phases to make these assessments of progress, and in some cases these will be crucial if later stages are dependent on knowledge, understanding or skills being established before next steps can be taken. Figure 1.2 shows a lesson planning template, different from the one used by Arthur, which embeds opportunities to gauge progress, while Figure 1.3 presents questions to guide your decision-making and judgement when planning with progress in mind.

Group	Date		Time
Focus of lesson in 'pupil speak' *Express as simply as possible*			
Learning objectives	Teacher versions:		*Pupil versions on slides / board*
Outcomes/main means of assessing learning			
Assessment data informing intention for progress …	From here …	To here …	

Phase	Time	Purpose of phase (build towards learning objectives)	What I do / what pupils do – describe activity and use of resources *Signal differentiation where relevant*	Progress interventions / checks

Figure 1.2   English lesson planning format

Around the topic or text

1. Am I clear on the curriculum focus for teaching? *Reading, Writing or Spoken Language?*

2. Do I know where pupils start from (a) collectively (b) as individuals? *>> use attainment data*

3. Am I clear about what constitutes **progress** here? *i.e. What is the next step for pupils?*

Challenge of the topic or text

4. Do I know where the challenge of the text or topic lies?
Conceptual? Of vocabulary? Of form? Requiring emotional maturity? etc.

5. Which precise features of language or text are key to progress? Where do I plan to address them?

6. Do I need to introduce details of the communication context of these features?

e.g. Are features used for a unique purpose, for a specific audience, or according to genre conventions?

7. How do I ensure pupils understand what is complex or distinctive about this?

8. Do I plan for pupils to develop and use vocabulary particular to these features?

Learning objectives	Responses and outcomes
9. Does the emphasis of the objectives reflect the area for learning? (Reading, Writing or Spoken Language)	In English, often a verbal expression of learning
10. Can I express precisely the relevant knowledge, skills and understanding in my objectives?	16. What sort of progress do I seek and what responses/outcomes show me that pupils make progress?
11. Can I articulate the objectives clearly for pupils in the format required by my school and department?	17. Have I designed activities sufficiently well to gain response /outcomes that are
12. If I look at learning objectives from one lesson to the next, and across the scheme of work, do they show progress in learning?	not subject to undue 'interference' from other thinking/use of language? Are they really a good means of gauging progress?
13. Do the objectives reflect progress *within* the lesson? (steps 1>2>3 increasing in difficulty, or step 1+2+3 = 4, steps combined in more complex final task)	18. Do I guide pupils enough (modelling) for them to use the required outcome format confidently?
14. Of all my objectives, which one is the most important and needs most emphasis in the lesson? (time allowed, nature of outcome)	19. Do the outcomes allow me to know who has made **progress**, and to what extent?
15. Against which objective do I most want to gauge **progress** in the plenary phase?	

Whole-class plenary phases

20. What progress do I want to check via the plenary? Against which objective? Best time?

21. Which precise features of language/text do I need to focus on? Is there a related key question?

22. Does the approach make the best use of time? Do I draw as much information as possible?

23. Who am I assessing? All or selected pupils? How to choose them?

24. Do I want my plenary to show or emphasise something for the whole class?

25. Should the plenary bring neat closure, or should it open questions for further learning?

Figure 1.3   Planning English lessons for progress: teacher's diagnostic device

Conclusion: what should your lesson design do?

The purposes of lesson design during initial teacher education differ from those for experienced teachers, especially over the very early stages of your course such as during a first school placement. When designing lessons for the first time you may find it difficult to shape appropriate learning objectives. It can also be challenging to make the lesson coherent so that activities match well with the learning objectives. During teaching, you may find you do not communicate the purpose of the lesson or activity to pupils as clearly as you had hoped. It is common in early lessons to struggle with 'signposting' the structure of the lesson well for pupils through your talk or resources.

For the beginning teacher, then, the process of lesson design helps develop understanding of the elements which support learning for pupils. It should also provide support for teaching during the lesson, acting as a reminder of sequence, key instructions and likely timing. With a lesson design committed to paper, it becomes easier for experienced teachers to help you bring coherence to lesson designs and ultimately to help you communicate this to pupils. It can give them insight into your thinking about pupils' learning; what will be achieved as a result of teaching, especially in the lesson objectives and outcomes; the purpose of separate phases; the introduction, development and articulation of concepts (and thus your subject knowledge); when and how to assess; the relationship between different parts of the lesson; and organisation of time and resources. What you include or omit also suggests to them your awareness of potential problems. In all these respects, a lesson design constitutes a diagnostic device, and allows those working with you to distinguish very clearly between the quality of your thought and your capacity to realise your ideas during teaching. As you might anticipate, your excellent ideas do not always find successful outcomes, so it helps training staff to see where and how to guide you.

Designing lessons also supports your capacity to articulate the rationale for your practice, an essential professional skill in its own right when communicating with parents, other colleagues and sometimes appraisers or inspectors of your work. After teaching any lesson there will be opportunity to refine your expression of learning objectives simply be revisiting them and rewording them if necessary. You will have the benefit of hindsight, weighing what actually happened against what you intended in the design. To what extent were you able to realise your intentions, and what aspects required change or deviation during teaching? Attention to the latter means that, over time, your lesson designs become increasingly realistic and likely to succeed: the frequency with which pupils learn what you want them to learn improves and with it the impact of your teaching. Ultimately, the lesson design is a bridge between your thought as a teacher, also made public to others, and your action in the classroom.

Website

Ofqual: http://ofqual.gov.uk/

References

Bruner, Jerome S. (1966) *Toward a Theory of Instruction*. Cambridge, MA: Belknap Press of Harvard University.

DfE (2011) *Teachers' Standards*. Reference: DFE-00066-2011.

DfE (2013) *English Programmes of Study: Key Stage 3 (National Curriculum in England)*. Reference: DFE-00184-2013.

DfE (2014a) *English Programmes of Study: Key Stage 4 (National Curriculum in England)*. Reference: DFE-00497-2014.

DfE (2014b) National Curriculum and Assessment from September 2014: Information for Schools. Online at: http://www.gov.uk/government/publications/national-curriculum-and-assessment-information-for-schools). (accessed 1 October 2014)

Gagné, Robert (1970) *The Conditions of Learning*, 2nd edn. London: Holt, Rinehart & Winston.

Ofqual (2013) *Reforms to GCSEs in England from 2015: Summary*. Coventry and Belfast: Ofqual.

Shakespeare, W. (2005) *Romeo and Juliet*. Oxford: Oxford University Press.

CHAPTER 2

READING A SET TEXT

Objectives of this chapter:

- To consider the convention of reading set texts in English, including novels and plays
- To explore different approaches to presenting and reflecting on set texts in class
- To reflect on the potential and limitations of various approaches to reading in class
- To reflect on the links between your chosen approach to reading and pupils' understanding of and response to set texts

---

Introduction

Picture thirty pupils, each turning a page in their own copy of a novel similarly held by others. Their movement is uniform, synchronised, while the teacher utters without pause the words that span the pages. Eyes move down the text – *how much are they really looking?* – and the process continues for minutes, in future lessons, the next term, year after year.

Reading a novel in class is perhaps *the* iconic and defining activity of English as a secondary school discipline, at least in the public imagination and in film. Robin Williams leads his pupils in a sort of print-based alchemy in *Dead Poets' Society*, and in *Kes* reading in class constitutes some of pupil Billy's space for refuge. If the impact of reading in class as epiphany is challenging to match in day-to-day practice, there are less positive representations. Reading in class can be media shorthand for tedium or tyranny, or just the last resort of the ill-prepared teacher. After all, if that's what English teaching is about, anyone could do it, surely? In most cases, whether done well or not, this form of reading happens without major incident and time passes one way or another.

Any teacher of English is likely to read texts with their classes on a weekly basis. The capacity to conduct the activity well, somewhere between the two caricature extremes, is a core skill. It is not, however, a competence identified explicitly in the core professional standards for teachers, nor is it easy to find professional development training focused on the skill. This chapter presents three examples of student teachers reading to their classes, and explores the merits of their approaches and alternatives they might opt to use for different effect. You should find the discussion here suggests a repertoire of approaches that you could use in your own teaching, making an informed choice according to the aims of the collective reading.

Erica reading *Of Mice and Men* with a Year 10 class

Erica and her class are far into the novel and today's lesson deals with a key episode in the narrative. They are studying Chapter Four in which the childlike Lennie, brother of George, is provoked by Curley to violence. Lennie breaks Curley's hand. For Lennie, the actions are almost involuntary: he has little concept of what he is doing or its implications.

The classroom in which Erica works is arranged in three rows of desks, with two pupils at each one. They sit in boy-girl pairs where possible, and face the front of the room towards both the teacher and the interactive whiteboard. In today's lesson every pupil has access to their own copy of the novel. As Erica reads, some pupils choose to look to their books while others prefer to listen.

Erica's choice in reading is to present the whole chapter without planned pauses. She reads from the chapter's opening to the end without interrupting for discussion, presenting the text with little elaboration. She opts to do all the reading herself, and effectively performs the text with well-projected and often expressive reading. She is fortunate in her ability to mimic American accents, and convincingly differentiates the voices of characters so that pupils can *hear* the shifts in speaker in the dialogue as well as see them on the page. She also varies tone and volume so that the reading is dramatic, especially as she conveys the tension of circumstances and then the urgency of the fight and George's imperative to 'Let him have it Lennie!' Pupils are visibly engaged by the episode, insofar as they appear attentive and those that listen and look towards Erica notice her gestures too, the way she complements aspects of the text in her own movements and facial expressions.

James reading *The Boy in the Striped Pyjamas* with a Year 8 class

James has taken great care in preparing his teaching of this novel, mindful of its potential to distress pupils as it provides a child's view of life in a Nazi concentration camp during the Second World War. He has also recognised that the novel assumes a mature and sophisticated reader, one who must understand the significance of incidents and details where the character of Bruno may not. He is aware that the process of reading in class should both provide a secure, emotionally safe environment for his pupils to engage with the story, and that it is the means for him to support pupils' awareness of nuances in the narrative. This classroom reading is so much more than getting through the text: James sees it as opportunity to model perceptive and empathetic reading. It can be challenging to realise these goals in any public arena where participants offer varying degrees of interest, attentiveness, maturity and cooperation.

In his first lesson of reading the novel with his Year 8 pupils, he has several aims in mind. He wants the class to become interested in the story as they read Chapter One, and for everyone to note and understand details that will be important to the developing narrative. In particular, he wants all his pupils to recognise that Bruno is ignorant of his father's employment as a Nazi officer, and therefore oblivious to what such work might entail. Simultaneously he is also establishing the routine for reading a shared class novel in his classroom, setting the ground rules that will be as much a part of the success of the unit as the activities he builds around it. The combination of these aims shows very clearly how classroom management and organisation in English are linked to subject-based processes and strategies for learning. In this case they are not an afterthought, rather they are subsumed into a view of reading in school as a collective and public activity which stimulates responses that though personal are mediated in a social and institutional context. Somehow that engagement and response must be ordered and guided, but the orderliness of the process is not the main purpose.

On the face of it, James' approach to reading the novel looks very similar to what Erica did. Similarly he opts to read himself and does so expressively, where appropriate. Unlike the *Of Mice and Men* chapter, however, this communicates a relatively low-key event. Where Erica's reading described an event of violent action, this expository passage describes Bruno discovering the family maid as she packs his belongings in a suitcase. He does not know why, and it is through the direct speech of his questions that James can convey the drama of the episode. James has made one very significant choice that means the way pupils experience the text in his class is very different to what happens in Erica's. He does not give his pupils copies of the book, so they cannot follow word-for-word as he reads. Instead, he requires only that they listen, both to the story he reads aloud to them and then to the brief prompts and questions he uses to punctuate the narrative. His first pause is midway through page 3, when Bruno's mother explains that the whole family is moving away, 'All four of us'. James simply stops and asks his pupils to 'Just think how Bruno might feel. Perhaps you remember a similar situation yourself.' He then resumes the reading: 'Bruno thought about this and frowned.' Half-way down the next page he pauses again where the narrator explains that Bruno 'wasn't entirely sure' what his father did for a living. James asks the class 'What do we know about Bruno's father so far?' and this time elicits comment from two pupils who note that he has a 'special job' and also, according to details on the first page, that maybe he doesn't treat the maid well.

Max reading *Macbeth* with a Year 10 class

Max is introducing his class to *Macbeth* for the first time. The group read Act 1, scene 1 in the first part of the lesson and are now reading the second scene. In this classroom, pupils sit around six bases (usually two tables pushed together to form a square) with five or six pupils at each. The initial impression is that the layout supports exchanges across groups. The pattern of reading Max has adopted is to select some pupils as readers, each taking a part. There are six speaking parts in the scene, though there are more characters described in the stage notes. Initially, King Duncan, Malcolm, Donalbain and Lennox enter (each of whom speak), together with attendants (who remain silent). The stage directions describe them 'meeting a bleeding Sergeant', who also speaks. Later Ross and Angus enter, though only Ross speaks.

Max designates the roles, with some pupils signalling enthusiasm through a valedictory 'Yes!' and others appearing neutral though not refusing. The first pupil reads Duncan's lines with fluency and clarity, flowing between lines 2 and 3:

1. What bloody man is that? He can report,
2. As seemeth by his plight, of the revolt
3. The newest state.

The second pupil reading Malcolm projects well but it is less fluent, pausing at the end of each line:

This is the sergeant
4. Who like a good and hardy soldier fought
5. 'Gainst my captivity. Hail, brave friend!
6. Say to the king the knowledge of the broil
7. As thou didst leave it.

When the pupil reads line 6, his tone and faltering fluency suggest that he has lost the sense of the lines himself, though he continues.

It is the pupil who reads these lines of the sergeant who struggles most obviously:

Doubtful it stood;
8. As two spent swimmers, that do cling together
9. And choke their art. The merciless Macdonwald –
10. Worthy to be a rebel, for to that
11. The multiplying villanies of nature
12. Do swarm upon him – from the Western Isles
13. Of kerns and gallowglasses is supplied;
14. And Fortune, on his damned quarrel smiling,
15. Show'd like a rebel's whore. But all's too weak;
16. For brave Macbeth – well he deserves that name –
17. Disdaining Fortune, with his brandish'd steel,
18. Which smoked with bloody execution,
19. Like valour's minion carved out his passage
20. Till he faced the slave;
21. Which ne'er shook hands, nor bade farewell to him,
22. Till he unseam'd him from the nave to the chops,
23. And fix'd his head upon our battlements.

The pupil pauses at each detail of punctuation, and makes a markedly longer pause for hyphens. Though the punctuation on the page creates a staccato effect, the pupil's reading is so faltering that sense is lost. The difficulties are compounded when the pupil encounters unfamiliar vocabulary ('Macdonwald', 'gallowglasses', 'minion'), to the extent that at one point the pupil stops out of frustration. It is only the encouragement of Max ('you're doing well') that ensures the pupil finishes. Max signals that he will read the next lines for the Sergeant, and the pupil seems relieved. The same problems are encountered across the rest of the scene and the overall effect is to lend the reading a sense of struggle. Pupils who generally respond well to Max's teaching seem tetchy, as if this process is something to be endured.

Options for Erica – responding to an observer's feedback

Erica's lesson went well and her reading of the passage from *Of Mice and Men* was engaging for pupils. A description of the form of reading activity could be as concise as 'the teacher reads the entire text – pupils follow in their own books'. After acknowledging the numerous strengths of her teaching in the lesson, observer feedback aimed to help Erica extend her repertoire of reading strategies. She received the following comments in written notes:

> Your reading of the text to pupils was impressive. Your expressiveness clearly engaged pupils and meant that the episode was inherently entertaining. The drama of events was very apparent through the fluency of your reading, emphasis of various words, and the timely pauses you introduced where appropriate. In all these aspects, your reading could be said to provide a model for pupils – an example of what good reading aloud sounds like. Your expressiveness is important for other reasons too: it acts as a cue which pupils do not have in the printed text, helping them make sense of what happens here. Though the fight is dramatic, there are subtle details that could be missed without adequate cueing. Your varying emphasis helped in this respect.
>
> One thing to note and to manage strategically is pupils' activity during reading. You were happy to let them read from the page or to simply listen. This will often be an appropriate approach, and you might want to signal the choice for the class overtly. At other times you might prefer to specify what they do. If you are reading an

extract which benefits from visualisation, perhaps because of how a character's appearance is described or a location evoked, listening may be preferable. If, however, you are reading a text prior to structural analysis, or simply one that introduces unfamiliar vocabulary in any quantity, the links between what is heard and seen may help pupils' in their work. In the latter respect, when you read aloud you are supporting decoding for them so introduce pronunciation to match what they see on the page.

Options for James – a discussion after teaching

In conversation with his tutor, James wanted to consider the response of pupils to the first chapter of *The Boy in the Striped Pyjamas*. Were pupils engaged in the story? Did they appear to recognise that Bruno knows very little about his father's occupation?

His tutor asked about their engagement – how did it compare with what James has encountered when pupils follow reading on the page, from a photocopy or a book?

James feels that his choice to read with pupils listening worked well. First, he noticed that pupils seemed more attentive than usual, as if it compelled pupils to concentrate, perhaps because of the simplicity and indeed pleasure of just listening. He notes that he didn't lose time, as he has in other lessons, having to remind some to look at their books or to find the shared page. For his own part, he wonders if he read a little more slowly and with a little more expressiveness than usual, knowing that pupils did not have the support of the printed text. He also says that the margin notes he made in his copy helped the fluency of the reading phase a great deal. He could make confident progress in the sustained reading phase because he knew at which points he wanted to pause, and already had prompts and questions formulated. These helped to lend rhythm to what otherwise could have been a fairly formless 20-minute period of listening. His tutor observes that James' interjections kept pupils alert, helped them reflect on details and built empathy with Bruno. Some were more precisely directing, for example when James asked pupils to remark on what they knew of Bruno's father. James had shaped this with the intention that pupils would need to pick out details in the chapter that could otherwise be overlooked in the fluency of the reading, with attention also on the unfolding narrative. It would also draw attention to the fact that available details were in fact very limited. James was careful to ask that question just before Boyne makes the dearth of information even more apparent. In the passage that James read straight after his questions, Boyne makes clear that Bruno does not have the slightest idea what his father does by describing his discussion with school friends. He learns that they know exactly the profession of their fathers, but when asked to explain about his own, Bruno cannot.

James has made a very successful start to his reading of the novel with the class, using brief interjections that act as cues to pupils' responses. Sometimes they lead pupils to empathy, at others to visualisation or pre-diction. The quality of James' own reading is key here. He has been astute in identifying salient details that will need attention as the class study the novel in its entirety. He is pre-empting comprehension that may only develop weeks from now, gently giving pupils their way into the story. At the same time, his decision to read aloud also draws attention to some localised detail: in this chapter, the text's play of homophones 'Fury' for 'Führer' becomes more gentle, more intriguing.

Options for Max – planning for the next lesson and beyond

In discussion of his lesson with his tutor, Max described his frustration with the classroom reading of *Macbeth*. He is enthusiastic about the play himself but feels a little demoralised that the experience of reading it around the class doesn't seem to be engendering the same levels of inter-est in pupils. He also worries that they may not understand what they have been reading. The approach he used seems sensible enough given the study text has the form of a play. Of all the forms likely to be used in the English classroom, that of play script is the one which most openly invites participatory reading across multiple roles. Some novels invite it too, where they have plentiful dialogue. The teacher might read the nar-rating voice and involve pupils in reading dialogue designated according to characters. Sometimes pupils find it difficult to distinguish one char-acter from another, especially where the arrangement of direct speech on the page does not explicitly attribute utterances and the speaker must be inferred. Plays mark speakers very clearly, and for this reason some teachers choose play adaptations of novels for shared reading. As Max finds, however, that doesn't guarantee engaging reading.

Max responds to his tutor's question about what he hopes to achieve through the class reading by outlining his commitment to involve as many pupils in reading over the next few weeks. He sees the shared reading of the play as an instance of inclusion in action, he feels it should be available to everybody. He also comments on what he has learnt already about some pupils as readers: he can see how the reading process signals to him information about their confidence and fluency. Most of all he wants the reading to be enjoyable for the pupils, for them to enjoy the play and experience some its of tension and excitement.

There are at least a couple of variations on this participatory reading that could help Max keep hold of these principles. Given the layout of the room, one option is to give more responsibility to pupils working in groups. If he maintains a process to mirror the whole-class reading but instead devolves it to table-based groups, he can involve every pupil in the class in taking a role. This will create a very different classroom atmosphere, with six shared readings occurring simultaneously, but it diminishes the public awkwardness that some pupils may feel reading (or indeed listening) in the peer-to-public whole-class setting. It also gives a little space for pupils to pause and explain things to one another or for Max to visit tables where he feels pupils may need assistance or direction. In terms of pupils' self-esteem, the potential for embarrassment is reduced. Of course, this new approach has its own limitations and demerits, and its success could relate to space, available support from assistants, pupil groupings and dynamics, even the acoustics of the room. The possibility of its positive impact might be improved with some form of induction to reading play scripts, and it will need familiarity over time to become established. As we have seen, the more conventional and established approach was no guarantee of effective reading, so Max might persevere with this new option or at least introduce it where scenes afford multiple roles.

A further, more systematic, variation on this strategy is for Max to organise activity so that pupils at each table have time to familiarise themselves with an allocated chapter, preparing a reading that they will share with the rest of the class. The approach works well with successive chapters or episodes and in poetry with stanzas. Again, the group phase requires all pupils take a part. In collaboration pupils are likely to assist each other in comprehension and interpretation of the text. Indeed, understanding may develop concurrently as they make decisions on what voices to adopt, where to place stress and where to pause, even where they choose to transfer the speaking role from one pupil to another. The teacher is freed to help weaker groups and the potential embarrassment pupils could experience at having to read (and make mistakes) publicly and alone is reduced in these more intimate groupings. To exploit the approach to its full potential, Max needs to exercise judgement about which parts of the play might benefit from this arrangement. He may find successive short scenes, where the distribution of reading in this way can underline the different mood or focus of each. Alternatively, the strategy may introduce variation to reading a lengthy scene, though the scope for distribution of sections to underline shifts could apply here too: perhaps it highlights transitions from one exchange to another involving different characters, or in more analytic mode to mark a change from a richly figurative soliloquy to a subsequent passage of rapid stage action. These approaches to shared reading offer variation but are more than that. Used with subtlety they are a resource for Max to make features of the text more apparent for pupils, to aid their comprehension and assist their recollection of events, features of language and structure.

Lesson structure and the practical matter of getting through a substantial text

The rhythm of reading a text in class is briefly touched upon in the account of James' lesson. Whatever approach these students choose from one lesson to the next, one inescapable fact of teaching substantial literary texts is the sheer amount of class time needed to read a text to completion. Early in planning, each student teacher needs to identify how many lessons or hours are available for teaching their text. Once they have the total, they also need to accommodate time for activities and sharing responses, as well as space for fostering writing skills. These should match the form of assessment required by their immediate curricular frameworks but ideally will prepare pupils for writing in other contexts as well.

In estimating the class time needed to 'get through' the text, you will need to work out how long it takes to read a single page aloud, and then calculate what proportion of a lesson is needed to read a chapter or the episode for the day. Timings will invariably need extending if reading aloud is to be shared by pupils as well, anticipating the organisation and encouragement of pupil speakers. Beyond the time necessary to read the text, there is the balance of the lesson. In some cases you may want to devote the full lesson to reading to build momentum and engagement, not forgetting the possible inherent pleasure of the narrative itself. In other cases, perhaps even as a matter of department policy, the lesson may fall into two parts of reading then linked activity, or take a structure of alternating reading with brief response activities. Given some of the approaches suggested earlier in this chapter, the lesson structure will depend to some degree on what type of reading is organised. In the case of Max's lesson, reading is guided and closely linked with response in a manner not easily captured in more conventional whole-class readings.

Reflection: when you think about it, it's a strange thing to do

Each of the examples above has described an approach to reading a text in a classroom setting. Though Erica, James and Max are each teaching classes, they are also guiding pupils as individuals to respond to and in most cases write about the study texts for attention. At some point soon, if not already, all of their pupils will have to articulate these responses in formally assessed work.

Whenever a teacher of English plans an approach to a shared class text, they are also planning to form a bridge between public activity and each pupil's private encounter with a text. If we stop to dwell on the activity of 'reading a class text', especially when it is a novel, the convention is an odd one. For obvious reasons, reading in this way is very different from how most of us would choose to read for pleasure. If we read at home, we might seek a quiet spot, a comfy chair, and identify a period when we can read for some time, uninterrupted. Otherwise, we might read with music in the background, perhaps while travelling on a train or bus. Even in these public settings, a book or tablet and perhaps music via headphones too serve to isolate us in our reading activity. In none of these cases do we encounter the text communally and simultaneously with others.

For parallels there we must look to cinema, or live performance, which we generally choose. The experience of 'reading in class' is a unique phenomenon, and one in which the social and institutional experience is nevertheless only tenuously linked to the usual mode of required response in formal writing. That means that if it is to be successful in both preparing pupils for the rigours of assessment and engaging them in pleasurable reading, the teacher must make careful choices at all stages of the process.

Where there is flexibility open to the teacher, it is sensible to consider the 'teachability' of any text. To what extent does it lend itself to communal reading, in an institutional setting, within a specified timeframe and for prescribed assessment goals? As it does any of these things, how far is it likely to interest, entertain and stimulate the young people upon whom it is imposed? Features of texts to be considered in these pragmatic deliberations include overall length, structure and narrative technique. Some novels or plays are structured such that the succession and pace of episodes lend themselves to classroom work, so that a key episode can become the focus of every lesson. Others will have chapters that can be read and considered within the duration of a single lesson. Whatever their other merits, in this alone they can suggest a sense of progress combined with satisfactory completion of one stage at a time. Other texts provide opportunities to exploit in a public forum: they have a distinctive and fluent narrator that replicates a spoken voice, sometimes capturing dialect or accent or both, and hearing this read well lends a new dimension to the reading experience. In other examples, there are multiple characters with dialogue, or in plays, roles where speaking parts can be distributed and the distinction in reading voices aids comprehension.

Yet others may combine action with subtlety and craft. It is no coincidence that *Of Mice and Men* has been so widely taught, or that it remained a staple of examination specifications until Michael Gove recommended its removal from specifications in 2014. It demonstrates most of these features, meaning the whole text can be experienced in the classroom, with time remaining for reflection, analysis and the development of the writing skills pupils need to convey their responses cogently and clearly on paper. By contrast, there are texts that the teacher might recognise from the outset can never be dealt with in their entirety in classroom time, in which case judgements about what *should* be covered during lessons may be influenced by similar characteristics. Which episodes need to be shared to offer a common feeling for plot and character? Which lend themselves to public discussion, where perspectives and interpretations may diverge?

One approach we haven't mentioned yet is the option to ask pupils to read parts of the text quietly and privately, in a manner more akin to reading for pleasure and leisure. If we take James' work around *The Boy in the Striped Pyjamas* as an example, he may decide that further into the text he wants to depart from the communal reading. There may be chapters around which he sustains the quality of his prompting and questioning, where they are instead collated on the whiteboard or a worksheet prior to a sustained silent reading period. It is entirely at his discretion whether the pupils answer the questions in writing, in the mode of traditional comprehension exercises, or whether he asks them to share their responses with a neighbour or more publically across the class. It is just one strategy of many available to him, one which can be embedded in the predominant approach of public reading, but which can be employed for extracts in texts where individual attention is especially important. With *The Boy in the Striped Pyjamas*, or indeed any emotionally demanding text, these might be the chapters that make affective demands of pupils, that have an impact best felt alone than in the sway of public feeling, the consensus interpretations that classroom readings can distil and consolidate. The teacher does retain some agency to offer pupils a partially private space and time for their own thoughts.

Conclusion: a wider ethos for reading in class

These approaches give the individual teacher choice, though whether used alone or in combination they comprise no more than a repertoire of strategies. They can support but not substitute the teacher's long view of what reading in class is intended to achieve, which is often far more than the response, however deep, to the immediate study text. The ethos for reading that Erica, James and Max want to create and convey will not necessarily be observable in a single lesson. It will develop over time, realised through their decisions across a full academic year. Beyond the early months of training to teach, it will take form within the context of departments, where first they will conform to policies and in time shape them. When they contribute to plans for teaching that span whole years and courses, from the first term for Year 7 to exam practice for Year 11 or an A-level group, the values that inform these early lessons will see their most complete form.

References

Boyne, John (2006) *The Boy in the Striped Pyjamas*. London: Random House.
Shakespeare, W. (1606/2005) *Macbeth*. Cambridge: Cambridge School Shakespeare.
Steinbeck, John (1937) *Of Mice and Men*. London: Penguin.

CHAPTER 3

ANALYSING LITERARY TEXTS

Objectives of this chapter:

- To consider the demands of literary analysis and some of the associated conventions such as using quotations
- To recognise the distinctiveness of texts and how to accommodate such distinctiveness in your approach to teaching
- To identify means of shaping precise learning objectives tailored to the study text
- To introduce simple means to help pupils through attention to the author's presentation of information for readers

---

Introduction

This chapter is about the study of literary texts with classes, and about supporting pupils with reading that contributes to written analysis of those texts. As such, it is about a very particular form of reading. It is reading which differs from reading for pleasure or reading in other disciplines. It is distinctive to literary study in that the text for scrutiny becomes an artefact for contemplation, just as a painting or sculpture might be, and where appreciation of its craftedness and aesthetic design becomes relevant. The literary text is what James Britton (1972: 247) called an instance of 'poetic' use of language, though he intended the term to mean far more than poetry alone. Because language is shaped in this very deliberate, patterned manner it differs from the 'expressive' uses of everyday communication, or the purposeful (or 'transactional') uses of non-fiction texts, which set out to influence thought or action but where aesthetic matters are of far less significance.

In secondary English teaching, pupils usually need to demonstrate their literary reading through written response. Conventionally, this entails the identification of quotations that support statements they wish to make about the texts. Usually this comment has to show that they are aware of the aesthetic organisation of the text, a domain summed up in curricular documents in phrases such as 'the author's craft' and evident in examination questions which require pupils to remark upon the author's 'presentation' of characters, ideas or themes.

Owen is engaging his class in exactly this sort of work here. He is teaching a lesson about characterisation in the novel the class is reading. It could be any novel, commonplace as this process is in English classes, but in this instance he is working with *Great Expectations* by Charles Dickens. In particular, his lesson is intended to help pupils 'understand how the author uses language to help readers imagine his characters'.

Owen has very good practical teaching skills. He can teach to his plan, has a good rapport with the group and is clear in the detail of his communication throughout the lesson. His lesson sequence seems logical too. He chooses to focus on the author's use of adjectives in an extract from the novel of around three hundred words. Before reading it with pupils he asks them to look at a few images of people (not from the novel) displayed via the interactive whiteboard, and to suggest adjectives to describe them. Pupils can refer to thesauri too if they wish as a means to offer greater variety in the range of adjectives suggested. After this activity he presents them with the extract drawn from the novel and with prompts that guide them to identify adjectives in the text, then to shape written paragraphs that convey how language helps readers imagine the characters. They are to use the convention of point-evidence-explain paragraphs and make reference to adjectives in particular. Pupils remain on task for the full lesson, and all manage to complete a paragraph relevant to the given task.

The outline here will be recognisable to many teachers of English, following a sequence of pre-task orientation with consolidation of the key term (adjective), a stage of application and then completion of an extended point-evidence-explain paragraph.

Tailoring learning objectives

The generalisable nature of the lesson sequence and Owen's apparent success in realising it in practice can distract us from aspects of teaching and learning that are subtle yet pivotal in the quality and depth of learning for pupils. The elements that matter are those that mean that 'off-the-peg' templates for teaching English have only limited value: nuance is crucial.

The first aspect to consider is the core learning objective and the implications that follow, a matter pertinent to any teaching and any other objectives that might apply. The second aspect is more special to English and literary study and concerns what is distinctive about the literary text (or extract of text) under scrutiny. The combination of a particular objective with a particular extract of text should give rise to a unique learning experience. Though a teacher may work from the same objective again, if they were to use it in connection with a different text, the lesson and learning outcomes must differ if pupils are to understand how language is used with any real attentiveness or subtlety.

Unique learning encounters such as those proposed here have resonance with Margaret Meek's summary of the reading process:

> ... in an act of reading what someone has written, we enter into a kind of social relationship with the writer who has something to tell us or something to make with words or language. The reader takes on this relationship, which may feel like listening, but is in fact different in that it is more active. He recreates the meaning by processing the text at his own speed and in his own way. As he brings the text to life, he casts back and forth in his head for connections between what he is reading and what he already knows. He pauses, rushes on, selects from his memory whatever relates the meaning to his experience or his earlier reading, in a rich and complex system of to-ing and fro-ing in his head, storing, reworking, understanding or being puzzled. (Meek 1982: 21)

The job of Owen, or any teacher of English, involves helping pupils become immersed in the same process and to develop the skills to resolve those moments of puzzlement. An additional observation by

Meek will inform some of the discussion here, that 'some successful readers say that they feel they are helping to create the work *with* the author'. It seems very pertinent when we have a learning objective concerning an author's use of language and the way it works on a reader's imagination.

Reflecting on the learning objective

Let us look at Owen's core objective once more: to understand how the author uses language to help readers imagine his characters. It looks and feels like a good English objective, and seems authentic. If we unravel it, now with Meek's summary of reading in mind, we will see it is also very challenging, building from a number of assumptions.

Taking 'how the author uses language' as the first component, what sort of understanding does this entail for pupils? First of all it will need them to have knowledge of relevant language resources at an author's disposal. The terms of the objective do not specify whether these resources are limited to 'word-level' (that is to say identifiable in single words, labelled by word class), 'sentence-level' (for example, choice of sentence type) or even 'text-level' (patterns or variations in language use across the entire piece). Attention to just one or all concurrently may be valid, but whatever the teacher's intention, the detail of what they have in mind has relevance to the nature and focus of teaching activities and to their sequence. Of course, the aspects of language available for study will also be particular to the text in hand. Finally, the teacher's means of gauging progress in learning will need to correspond to the selected items of language use for consideration. Clearly, there is more chance of making a meaningful, precise and accurate assessment of progress if the items of language use for focus are clearly identified at the outset. If each level of language use is to be considered, would a point-evidence-explain paragraph offer pupils the structure to describe each and their various effects? Whatever the level chosen, pupils will need to be introduced to the aspects of language use and work with the related items. If, for instance, they are indeed focused on word-level detail, which verbs, nouns, adverbs or adjectives (to identify only a few) are most relevant to the text for study?

Within this same component of the objective, we find reference too to 'the author'. Whether or not the teacher chooses to name the author, it is clear that pupils are expected to appreciate that the language they read is not 'given' but that someone has constructed and crafted it making choices about their use of language. Likewise, the latter part of the objective recognises an abstracted 'reader'. Implicit in learning according to this objective is an expectation that pupils conceive of a reader as a self-conscious agent. This also suggests that they may have a nascent awareness of reading as a cognitive process. Given that attention here is on how the use of language 'helps the reader imagine' characters, pupils need not only identify features of language that appear to them significant in the text, they must also explain their possible effects on readers' minds. Either way, pupils need to read in a way that is metacognitive and which needs them to be aware of their own comprehension. If the objective presents to them a notional 'reader', does this support that process more effectively than an objective framed with direct address: 'how language use helps *you* imagine the characters'? The benefits of each are unlikely to be fixed, their effectiveness instead dependent on the group and perhaps to their prior experience as analysts of literary texts.

The emphasis in the objective about how the reader is helped to 'imagine' also merits comment with regard to the thought processes that occur during reading. In what ways does any reader 'imagine' characters? Is it some process of visualisation, a film in the head? Or is it through some empathy with characters, shifting one to another as the reader makes their way through the pages? Perhaps there is no single means of 'imagining', different texts guiding our imaginations in different ways. If a text presents aspects of a character's appearance by itemising their features one by one, perhaps supplemented by adjectives, it may be likely to stimulate a visual image in our minds by virtue of its attention to details that would – if they existed in the material world – be concrete, tactile and observable. It may also evoke in our minds impressions of movement, through its use of verbs and adverbs. As soon as a text begins to make more figurative use of language, however, it may prompt imagining in a different way. By stimulating associations through simile or metaphor, it will be likely to foster responses that are less consistent in nature, built instead on the personal resonance of figurative details for individual readers. Further, depending on the nature of each metaphor or simile, these may appeal to a wider range of senses than those generally stimulated by literal description – because figurative uses tend to evoke complete, synaesthetic moments of experience rather than atomised, isolated details. If reference to the working of language on the imagination is part of an objective, pupils need the verbal tools themselves to be able to explain what adjectives might do, or what a given metaphor can do, and so there is scope in the lesson or a wider scheme to include work on the capacity of different uses of language to convey information: their affordance.

The distinctiveness of the text

If the objective itself suggests subtle details that require consideration in a lesson sequence, so does the text chosen for study and as the vehicle for looking at how language works on readers. Owen decided to focus especially on the language resources of adjectives, simile and metaphor and how they were used in this extract from *Great Expectations*:

> In an arm-chair, with an elbow resting on the table and her head leaning on that hand, sat the strangest lady I have ever seen, or shall ever see.
>
> She was dressed in rich materials – satins, and lace, and silks, – all of white. Her shoes were white. And she had a long white veil dependent from her hair, and she had bridal flowers in her hair, but her hair was white. Some bright jewels sparkled on her neck and on her hands, and some other jewels lay sparkling on the table. Dresses, less splendid than the dress she wore, and half-packed trunks, were scattered about. She had not quite finished dressing, for she had but one shoe on, – the other was on the table near her hand, – her veil was but half arranged, her watch and chain were not put on, and some lace for her bosom lay with those trinkets, and with her handkerchief, and gloves, and some flowers, and a Prayer-Book all confusedly heaped about the looking-glass.
>
> It was not in the first few moments, though I saw more of them in the first moments than might be supposed. But I saw that every-thing within my view which ought to be white, had been white long ago, and had lost its lustre and was faded and yellow. I saw that the bride within the bridal dress had withered like the dress, and like the flowers, and had no brightness left but the brightness of her sunken eyes. I saw that the dress had been put upon the rounded figure of a young woman, and that the figure upon which it now hung loose had shrunk to skin and bone. Once, I had been taken to see some ghastly waxwork at the Fair, representing I know not what impossible personage lying in state. Once, I had been taken to one of our old marsh churches to see a skeleton in the ashes of a rich dress that had been dug out of a vault under the church pave-ment. Now, waxwork and skeleton seemed to have dark eyes that moved and looked at me. I should have cried out, if I could.
> (Charles Dickens, *Great Expectations*, 1860)

Although we see at first glance that it is quite easy to find adjectives in the extract, consistent with the salient aspect of language Owen nominated for analysis, very few of them actually describe Miss Havisham directly. First we have 'the strangest lady', then learn that 'her hair was white'. Later, we find 'her sunken eyes', 'the rounded figure of a young woman' and 'dark eyes' – and that is all. The majority of remaining adjectives apply to her jewels or clothing. Where we do find adjectives applying to her, they are rarely straightforward. 'Strangest' is in the superlative form and may not be as readily identified as an adjective by pupils as 'strange' might be. Three of the other four describe items conventionally subsumed into descriptions of appearance, hair and eyes, but the final 'dark eyes' belong to Miss Havisham transformed in metaphor to 'waxwork and skeleton'. Pupils have to recognise that this metaphor refers to Miss Havisham before they can accurately identify that the adjective is attributed to her eyes. Similarly, 'the rounded figure of a young woman' is a previous Miss Havisham imagined by Pip, not the one present before him. Elsewhere, when adjectives apply to clothing and jewellery, they are quite limited in range: *rich, white* (× 4), *bright, splendid* and the compound (again tricky for pupils?) *half-arranged*. That *white* is used four times may be more interesting and salient than the adjectives more generally.

This is not to say it is not useful to consider the adjectives used, but it may be helpful at least to ask pupils to sort them into groups: those that describe Miss Havisham's bodily appearance and those that describe her clothing and accessories. Further, a useful diagnostic category from the teacher's perspective would be one to hold adjectives that pupils find puzzling or difficult to sort. This provides a mechanism that legitimises 'problem' cases for discussion and frames activity so that pupils do not feel their lack of comprehension as a deficit. In the context of the lesson as a whole this can be the basis for a planned opportunity for the teacher to explore with pupils items that demonstrate language use that is complex or subtle, usefully consistent with the core objective.

Further discussion

There are other approaches available to Owen beyond attention to the single word-class of adjectives or to the literary techniques of simile and metaphor. In starting with these items (and it is easy for a beginning teacher of English to feel that this is what they should be doing) perhaps he has been distracted from what is individual to the text and what it does that is unique. In turn, this can mean that some very simple ways of helping pupils think about language use can be overlooked.

Identifying distinctive aspects of the study text: example

The first thing that strikes me when I read the extract from *Great Expectations* is that everything I learn is mediated by Pip. Furthermore, variations of 'I saw' or 'I have seen' are repeated across the extract to such an extent that it seems more than coincidence. In the third paragraph especially, in which the voice of Pip says 'I saw' five times, it appears Dickens wants to draw our attention to the fact that what we see is what Pip sees, it is his field of vision and reaction to what is in it that we experience. So, in terms of language resources, I can note first person perspective and this particular repetition of seen/saw verbs as potentially useful pedagogically. Already this is a combination of text- and word-level elements.

I'm also aware that relative to quite meagre detail about Miss Havisham's physical appearance, I nevertheless have a lengthy inventory of her accessories and their location in her room. Just as a list of concrete nouns in sequence I have satins, lace, silks, shoes, veil, bridal flowers, jewels, some other jewels, dresses, half-packed trunks, one shoe, her watch and chain, some lace for her bosom, trinkets, handkerchief, gloves, some [more] flowers, and a prayer book. This list alone constitutes 19 separate items. Perhaps the possibility of discussing nouns is not considered by Owen because their use is perceived as somehow less an element of craft than selective use of adjectives, which in their grammatical function provide an addition, a dash of colour. Maybe, though, it is possible to think of means by which pupils reflect upon this list, this profusion of items and how it works on the imagination.

One thing attention to isolated words or techniques of a specified class won't allow pupils to do easily is comment on features of texts that extend beyond sentence boundaries. The third paragraph here presents us with Pip's train of thought, or more accurately how he reflects on his train of thought as the first sentence of the paragraph reveals. To comment on what he sees before him he has to imagine an earlier Miss Havisham and recognise that she has changed. The way he sees now is additionally informed by his own very personal memories that are not about Miss Havisham herself: his recollection of the fair and of an exhumed body seen in a marshland churchyard.

An alternative approach taking account of the distinctiveness of the text

If a teacher wishes pupils to understand how the author uses language to help readers imagine his characters, we can exploit the appeal to the imagination. In more prosaic terms, we are really working with a question about information. What information is provided for us that allows us to create in our minds an idea of a person to match this noun-phrase 'Miss Havisham'? A second step, once we identify the information (or forms of information) is to ask ourselves how we learn this information? With this focus on information it becomes possible to map strategies that can be applied to any number of literary texts.

For the first question about 'what information', it is entirely possible to answer in common-sense terms without reference to literary jargon. Framing for pupils, we might ask 'What do you know about Miss Havisham from this extract?' This allows responses that encompass concrete, stated detail, such as she has white shoes ('Her shoes were white'). It could also elicit a response such as 'she is old', which is true but not overtly stated. Here the first question dovetails with the second, as it becomes important then to ask 'how do you know that?' [that she is old]. By doing so we get to the heart of how language is used and to webs of meaning that shape our impressions without direct, blunt or limited expression. We can get to the detail of language by asking an individual pupil to explain which information or detail prompts that impression, or indeed asking everyone in the class to note three phrases that could contribute to the impression that she is old. Answers could include 'the bride … had withered', 'sunken eyes' and 'shrunk to skin and bone', though other selections would be valid. This latter step is a useful one as often the impressions shaped by language cannot be pinned down to isolated words or phrases, but instead occur because of the interplay between two or more. Nor do these examples demonstrate 'language use' of a common type. If we look at word-class, 'had withered' is a verb form, 'sunken' is an adjective and 'shrunk to skin and bone' a recognisable idiom. Significantly, classifying in this way tells us nothing of their effect on our imagination and therefore does not adequately assist pupils in explaining how language is used. At this juncture it could be valid to ask pupils how the phrases affect their thoughts and feelings. Because these examples describe visible phenomena (and visible to Pip), it would seem apt to ask 'what do you see in your head, in your mind's eye', and then to redirect them to the text: which phrase or few phrases are most important for creating that mental image? Given the objective, unless pupils are asked to articulate what they imagine in response to the text themselves, they have little chance of engaging with the assumption that the author's use of language had an influence on the imagination of anyone. As an aside, this also needs to be taken into account when preparing their initial encounter with the text. What mode of reading, and in what circumstances, is most likely to engage their imagination before tasks or analytic attention are prescribed?

Application

In summary, the principles outlined above can be generalised to apply to a range of texts while allowing for the fact that language is used in highly distinctive ways from one text to another. Though the teacher may be able to work from a generic list of prompts or questions, the greater part of their preparatory work will be in analysing the study text themselves. They will aim to recognise those features that are distinctive and salient to the text, so that what they find can inform the way in which they present the text to pupils, what they choose to ask pupils about, which features of language are most pertinent to address overtly and an appropriate sequence for doing all of these things.

Some possible general questions to shape an approach around the information readers receive about characters follow, together with a brief comment describing responses that could be anticipated and their contribution to learning:

1. *What information does the text give you about the character?* This permits an intuitive and 'common-sense' summary, which could involve direct quotation of information or paraphrased items. It may also elicit impressions which are correct but not stated directly in the text.

2. *We have shared examples of information. Can you think of ways to group the information into different types?* If there are differing forms of information, it may be apt to group them. This process could be left open following the question provided above, with pupils classifying as they see fit (a high-order thinking skill), or the teacher may wish to provide categories they consider suited to the text in hand. Perhaps there is information about what can be seen that could be further categorised according to characters or people, creatures, the place or setting and specific objects. Relevant word-classes are likely to include concrete nouns and verbs of action and movement, nuanced by adjectives and adverbs. Additionally there may be information about someone's thoughts or feelings, revealing the immediate psychology of characters in the episode and of the type not accessible in the actual world other than by inference or what others tell us of their inner thoughts. This may be shared with us in the text through dialogue or narrative perspective, but also in the interplay of any number of

phrases and a variety of language resources. Often, these will work across sentence-level and probably text-level also. Further, there may be information about things outside of the place or event immediately described, for instance the memories of the narrator evoked by what they see, and again this information might only make sense when the text is viewed as a whole. An example might be a text in a first-person voice that alternates between the narrator's engagement in current events (the narrator's present) and memories or prior events similarly described by that first-person voice. If a teacher wished to prompt pupils to reflect on such items they may need to ask only 'What do you know about when things are happening?'

3. A related question is: *How is the information given to you?* This can be guided by the teacher through presentation of different means by which information is conveyed. This principle can be built into teaching sequences across schemes of work or even an academic year, so that pupils build their confidence and repertoire of information types and means of presentation. Possible means of articulating ways in which information is conveyed include:

a. by the narrator and through the type of narrator (omniscient third person, first person, dual narrative);

b. through organisation of the text (in linear sequence? paragraphs or sections focused on different things?);

c. through what characters say and how they say it (in dialogue, and representations of dialect);

d. through descriptions of characters' thoughts (any means of conveying interior thought);

e. through direct and literal description of things in the world of the characters (perhaps use the analogy of photography?);

f. through figurative uses of language that may trigger imaginative or affective associations in individual readers, often through an appeal to the senses;

g. through selection and emphasis (is more text devoted to particular items, and are others given little attention?);

h. through contrasts (for instance, if we are introduced to two characters in the same chapter, do pupils feel they are led to empathise with one more than the other?);

i. through the combined effect of details over a piece (for instance, where there may be a number of phrases that suggest a character may be malign, which when accumulated leave the reader in no doubt).

Of course, the list is not intended as a rule book, it is merely an illustration of the ways you might conceive of information for presentation and discussion with pupils. The best result would be for pupils to add to the list. The point, ultimately, is that they can select from a repertoire of options that allow for precise comment on how language functions to work on the reader rather than floundering without any supporting frame of reference.

Conclusion

The only way to draw these principles into your teaching usefully is to take a text that you know you will be studying with pupils and identify its distinctive traits. Once that is done, it becomes possible to develop lines of questioning or sequences of activity that respond to its unique nature, even though the underlying core objective may be a generic one about language use. Additionally, I recommend supplementing the core objective with others that acknowledge what is particular to the text in hand. They are likely to be objectives that cannot be transferred by cut-and-pasting to other plans, but instead will be tailored to the text and no doubt what you know of the class too. In the case of Owen's lesson, we might add objectives like these, anticipating that pupils will:

1. identify and classify the different things Pip sees in Miss Havisham's room;
2. recognise what Pip sees in the present and how what he sees links with his memories;
3. explain the effect of Pip's perspective on their own impression of Miss Havisham.

Around each objective, Owen may feel he wants to introduce terms applicable to pinpointing uses of language, such as concrete nouns and lists (1) and first-person voice and verb tenses (2) so that they inform the spoken and written explanations (3). Crucially, identifying language resources does not drive the lesson or learning: instead the focus is on how language is used by the author and how it works on pupils.

You may want to apply the principles described in this chapter to a new extract, drawn from a novel you are due to work on with a class. Build your approach from a core objective paralleling Owen's own about *Great Expectations*, understand how the author uses language in this extract to help you imagine the character described, and try to develop your own supplementary objectives based on the approach illustrated above that recognise distinctive features of the text. They will signal to you the aspects that need attention in lesson time and around which you are likely to build activity. As with the example from *Great Expectations*, application to your own text requires your own careful consideration and analysis of the extract if you wish to support pupils in close engagement with the text and guide them towards intelligent, rigorous responses that go beyond formulaic expression.

References

Britton, James (1972) 'What's the use? A systematic account of language functions', in A. Cashdan and E. Grugeon (eds), *Language in Education*. London: Routledge/Open University Press.

Dickens, Charles (1860) *Great Expectations*. London: Penguin.

Meek, Margaret (1982) *Learning to Read*. London: Bodley Head.

CHAPTER 4

WRITING BASED ON LITERARY MODELS

Objectives of this chapter:

- To consider the connection between literary reading and creative writing
- To explore means of establishing a strong link between reading activity and the writing composed by pupils
- To recognise the complexity of working around the different skills of reading and writing
- To support you in maintaining a challenge for pupils while providing adequate support

Introduction

Jonah's lesson on writing a good opening paragraph for a story is the focus of this chapter. He shares with his class a number of examples from published prose narratives, such as the following:

There was no possibility of taking a walk that day. We had been wandering, indeed, in the leafless shrubbery an hour in the morning; but since dinner (Mrs. Reed, when there was no company, dined early) the cold winter wind had brought with it clouds so sombre, and a rain so penetrating, that further out-door exercise was now out of the question. (Charlotte Brontë, *Jane Eyre*)

How do you respond to this yourself? Take a moment to reflect. What impact does it have on your emotions, your mind's eye or your thinking? Further, if you are able to shape a self-aware description of its effect on you, how might that help you to write a beginning for a narrative yourself? These questions suggest something of the demands inherent in Jonah's lesson as he grapples with the complex process of bridging reading and writing.

Jonah's lesson on writing the opening for a story

Jonah begins his lesson by presenting to his class the opening sentences drawn from five novels. Pupils read the examples from the page, and Jonah asks them the question: 'Which do you think is most effective?' Initially, pupils are a little quiet, though Jonah has a good rapport with his pupils and coaxes comments from them. He then directs them more deliberately to identify features of the examples, usually eliciting comment that recognises the use of literary devices through terminology like 'alliteration'. On occasion, pupils refer to the way texts create a puzzle or mystery that might intrigue a reader.

After this identification of features that support 'effectiveness', Jonah asks his pupils to begin writing an opening paragraph for a story, specifying that they should do so on their own. After 15 minutes of writing, Jonah concludes the phase to give pupils time to consult one another on the effectiveness of their story openings. On his lesson plan he identifies this final phase as one of assessment for learning (see Black et al., 1990; Black and Wiliam, 1990; Assessment Reform Group, 2002), acknowledging the role of peers in shaping formative feedback.

The observation notes made by a tutor observing Jonah's lesson recognise several traits for him to sustain in his teaching, given their evident success. His thinking about what is likely to help pupils towards their own writing is sound. He understands that a key principle of such work is for pupils to see examples of interesting story openings, which can stimulate their thinking and provide them with instances where authors have used various techniques to hook the reader and convey important information. His text choices suggest he is aware of the textual and linguistic features of writing that require attention if pupils are to make use of a range of devices in their own work. In his questioning, he emphasised the function of the opening to provide key details for the reader that may have a bearing on later narrative development, prompting pupils to consider 'what information an opening could contain'. When pupils began to volunteer their ideas about the characteristics of an effective opening to a story, he responded with praise when some suggested a significant consideration to be how the writing affects you, or indeed any reader. The sequence of the lesson, building from models, through identification of textual features, to writing demonstrated his appreciation of processes acknowledged to be effective in research literature (Myhill, 2005; Wray et al., 2000). In addition, he saw an opportunity for pupils to support one another, appropriately framing it as assessment for learning. Jonah saw that his own perspective as the teacher was not the only one of value, and that pupils could support each other well by providing feedback. It is possible too that his use of such activity was informed by thinking that, by giving feedback to others, pupils also help themselves as writers (for a discussion of the merits of similar strategies, see Hawe and Dixon, 2014). They have to articulate the impact of writing, which might make it more prominent in their own mind when they resume composition themselves. Of course, these dimensions of subject expertise were not the only important characteristics that contributed to a successful lesson. Jonah's excellent relationship with his class meant that they seemed at ease in offering suggestions about what might constitute a good, 'effective' story opening, and all pupils settled quickly to quiet and focused writing when required. The smooth transition to the peer-feedback phase also indicated that Jonah had established and could maintain an environment where pupils conducted themselves with maturity and mutual respect. Without these circumstances, the judgements he made concerning literary reading and writing might diminish a great deal in their impact. The changes Jonah might make to his lesson and future teaching are subtle, more a matter of widening a repertoire of approaches than having to rework things entirely. The use of the terms 'effective' and its cognate 'effectiveness' deserves some consideration in the light of pupils' own comments about the impact of writing on reader, and if Jonah wants to extend his accommodation of pupils' opinions handled so well in the peer-evaluation phase. If Jonah or any teacher starts with the notion of 'effectiveness', does it have any objective measure? Whose 'effectiveness' are we discussing?

The issues arising from this lesson

Though Jonah's lesson is unrepeatable by others in so far as it has a sequence he has designed, uses texts he has chosen and is shaped to support the learning of a unique group of pupils with their own dynamic, it nevertheless has elements which he will need to address again in other areas of his teaching. In particular, there are matters of writing pedagogy that can apply across any composition work Jonah leads in future, and which will be relevant to other teachers as well. The requirements of the curriculum are sufficiently open to make similar work again a likely prospect, and certainly that comparable learning objectives will need to be addressed. The details for writing (DfE, 2013: 17) state that pupils will 'write accurately, fluently, effectively and at length for pleasure and information', for varying purposes and audiences, in stories and 'other imaginative writing'.

The first point for discussion can be framed very simply as a matter of head and heart. To what extent is it possible to combine analytic work with attention to emotions? The relationship between the two is implicit in the contribution of the pupil who felt that considering the effect of the opening on the reader, the impact of sentences, constituted relevant business in studying the sentences. Before pupils can analyse details and speak of their effectiveness or otherwise, they need to have felt the effects (or at least appreciate the possible effects) of words on the page. Analysis of any depth requires some engagement of feeling, some affective response as a foundation (see Krathwohl et al. (1971) on the affective dimensions of learning).

In this respect, Jonah's questioning around 'effectiveness' is problematic, though his inclination to use the word is understandable given its recurrence in examination questions that ask pupils to discuss the effectiveness of writing concentrating on one or two aspects of the author's craft. One example, for instance, asks pupils studying Diane Samuels' *Kindertransport* to respond to the conclusion of Act One: 'how effective do you find this ending?' (AQA, 2012: 7). The trouble with this notion of 'effectiveness' is that it assumes and imposes on the pupil a founding assumption that the study text is effective in whatever way is asserted by the question. If taken as a starting point for classroom discussion it is difficult for pupils to deal with, because they haven't had space even to articulate the sort of effects the text they read or heard might have on them, let alone evaluate their impact. It is quite possible that whatever they are attending to may not be 'effective' for some individuals, and this is probably a more accurate reflection of reading outside classrooms. Maybe there are teachers of English who do not find passages of some canonical literature 'effective' on a personal level.

Unfortunately some pupils may feel that where they do not find something effective but where the teacher takes effectiveness as given, the deficiency is their own rather than that of the text. It is this potentially alienating outcome, the exclusion of pupils from what Basil Bernstein called the 'elaborated code' (1973: 173) of classroom language, that we can try to avoid if we remain alert to it. And if the skill of describing and explaining the impact of words on readers, according to identifiable purposes, remains important, there may be more inclusive ways of getting there.

One of the most challenging strands of Jonah's lesson, though largely tacit until the pupil raised it, is for pupils to appreciate the impact on the reader. Without overt attention to readers, his interest in 'effectiveness' can only be partially successful at best. Even when mentioned explicitly, 'the reader' may be a difficult notion for pupils to grasp. It is an anonymous figure, an abstraction, unless Jonah can help pupils value their own reading responses and see themselves as the first reader that matters. What is the impact, the effect, of the text on them?

The next challenge in the sequence of the lesson is for pupils to use any insights they have gained about the effectiveness of story openings they have read to inform their writing. Jonah has to do the work of all English teachers: to help pupils make a bridge between reading and writing, between the models and their own compositions. How directing does the stimulus and scaffolded support need to be? How should Jonah guide pupils to a good quality of response, while preserving the freedom for pupils to be inventive in what is essentially a creative process? And how should he guide pupils to demonstrate particular uses of language, balancing this with suggesting to them material or content for their work?

At the end of the lesson, Jonah did include a phase which indicated his view that pupils can work autonomously. In peer-assessment he trusted them as readers of each other's work. Again, though, they gauged writing according to its 'effectiveness', and opportunity was missed to evaluate the writing, at the simplest level, as communication. Before addressing effectiveness, there could be room for pupils to find out what their writing provoked in others in terms of feelings, thoughts or ideas. Are these the outcomes that each pupil-author intends, or within a range that matches what they hope might be the outcome of their crafted language?

Responding to these points in teaching

Before we consider how Jonah might adapt his teaching in response to those issues, let us recognise what pupils are asked to do across the sequence of the lesson. The demands are many, but it is easier to recognise how challenging the lesson really is if we express the different cognitive domains (see Bloom et al., 1979: 7) they work in as a list:

- Recognise and articulate their own response as readers.
- Recognise the possible responses of notional readers/the abstracted 'reader'.
- Understand writing as communication, conveying ideas and emotions with impact on the reader.
- Recognise the relevant resources of written language and what they can do.
- Translate features of the story opening models to their own writing.
- Generate content for their writing.
- Craft their own writing for presentation in the form of a paragraph in prose.
- Evaluate the qualities of a peer's writing.

Jonah's lesson encompasses all of these to some extent, but through the pursuit of the 'effectiveness' of writing it obscures the reader, and thus to a degree each of the first three items are no more than tacitly acknowledged. By shifting the emphasis of his plan around these, Jonah could improve the quality of pupil writing and also the impact of peer feedback.

Recognising pupils as readers

If Jonah wants to foreground pupils as readers themselves, he can do this from the earliest stages of the lesson, both in his presentation of the model openings he provides for pupils and discussion around them.

In notes of feedback for Jonah, his tutor remarked that the very act of presentation could be essential to the quality and depth of pupils' engagement. The tutor recommended that Jonah should:

> Dwell on the shared texts a little longer so that the distinctiveness of each becomes more apparent. This could build from a very deliberate strategy when reading the examples aloud of uttering the first and final sentences emphatically. Your emphasis can act as a cue to pupils,

helping them notice important details and conveying tone which might not be obvious to all when read from the page. You can also give pupils an explicit prompt to visualise what the extracts describe where appropriate, something like 'Just think of that for a moment. What pictures come into your mind?'

This simple technique gently eases pupils into self-aware reading, but avoids use of abstractions such as 'effectiveness' and 'impact' which do not draw so directly on pupils' immediate and more intuitive responses. The underlying aim with these initial questions is to find some access to how any of the extracts have worked on pupils immediately, before their responses are mediated through the language of literary analysis. The tutor elaborates the point:

When sharing the story openings aloud, exploit your experience as a reader to make the most of the writing as sequence: it may build tension, a sentence may undercut what came before or there might be a shift in tone that can be clarified through a timely pause. Reading aloud can make pupils more aware of the differing rhythms, voices and stylistic features of the text.

Seeing these comments after the lesson, Jonah realised that if he read the extracts aloud at the start instead of asking pupils to read from the page, he could replicate the same change in what he asked of pupils. He suggested that if he were to begin the peer-assessment phase with pupil-authors reading their story openings aloud to a partner, the pupils listening could comment on the elements captured in a vocal reading. The pupil-author might read in a way that conveys the intended fluency, momentum or tone of the piece, even if they are not able to capture that on the page. The questions pupils address in the peer-evaluation phase need not start from the abstraction of 'effectiveness' but can instead build from the real responses of real readers. The technique preserves the writing as communication, and makes clear the connection between actual response and the work of a writer striving for an effect. Jonah could set up the peer-evaluation so that the pupil-author reads their work and afterwards the listener just describes an aspect of their response. The purpose of this is for the writer to gain a sense of the effect of their own writing, which may or may not be what they intended. It is the teacher's judgement whether to provide a directing point ('Describe the tone of what you heard', 'Tell the writer which details hooked you, and if anything was unclear'), or to leave it to the pupil-author to seek a response about an aspect of their choice. The technique also permits a second stage, where pupils move to discuss their writing as it is presented on the page. Where one pupil has first heard the work of another and thus grasped the general sense of the piece, they can be directed to thinking about how far the same sense is captured on the page. This could, for instance, involve looking carefully at the sequence in which key details are presented, or scrutinising the use of punctuation to see if it marks, say, pauses or the shifts between speakers in dialogue in a way that matches what they heard.

A final point that Jonah and his tutor discussed was the context for reading the extracts, and what scope there might be for drawing on pupils' experiences of prose narrative more broadly:

> Begin with simplicity. Ask pupils to recall a story that they enjoyed from the start, and/or start with an example of your own. Build from here with questions that guide pupils to draw out the features you have identified as being important in their analysis and later writing.

The extracts Jonah shared, or any selection, have the benefit of providing a focus for discussion. They offer a foundation for the lesson, reference points for all that follows. Yet the consideration of story openings is also an opportunity to do more than meet Jonah's lesson objectives. This sort of activity is a chance to recognise what is usually called 'wider reading' and 'reading for enjoyment' (National Literacy Trust, 2013). These dimensions of reading are often promoted in whole-school literacy initiatives. In this case Jonah has an opportunity to convey an ethos about reading and its value. Before presenting the extracts, or even before declaring to his class the learning objectives, Jonah could choose to help pupils 'tune in' to the lesson through what might at first appear to be casual questioning about what they are reading for pleasure. He can build on a general question by asking all pupils to recall a novel they have enjoyed and then about what hooked them, what gave them the motivation to continue reading it. Through this he might elicit examples drawn from a wider range of texts, and about texts which pupils already deem 'effective' given their continued reading of them. Jonah need not limit the gentle questioning to literary prose narratives, as he could find it serves his objectives to draw on narratives in other media, for instance from television or film. Over time, he can develop the skill to draw the parallels with prose narratives. By working through this dialogue, he ensures that any consideration of story openings and their impact is grounded in the responses pupils have already had as readers, so that any discussion about the effect of the extracts he has selected can be considered relative to the impact of examples in their own reading histories. It also permits discussion of the inevitable fact that what one reader finds effective another may not, legitimising comment about the times when pupils have not persisted with a novel because the opening did not grab them.

The story openings chosen by Jonah

As Jonah's discussion with his tutor continued, and arising from this thinking about pupil reading, Jonah also noticed something about the extracts he had presented to pupils. All of them were drawn from critically acclaimed and canonised texts of the sort that might well appear on GCSE, A-level or degree courses. On one hand, this addresses a requirement of the curriculum for English to expose pupils to texts of a high quality (see English curriculum for Key Stage 3, DfE, 2013: 3). However, as with the original approach to response and 'effectiveness', it risks separating the experience of pupils as readers from the reading and analysis of texts in their English classroom. The approach may subtly suggest to pupils that their own reading, the texts they like, are not ones valued in the subject of English, or worse still by their teacher. Jonah felt that in future he would prefer to provide extracts drawn both from critically established works, and from novels currently popular among his pupils and their age group. He could draw on shortlists such as the nominees for the Carnegie Medal awarded for outstanding books for children, or even incorporate recommendations identified by pupils and prepared by him prior to planning this lesson, for example if he became aware of 'buzz' texts in his class through regular library lessons. The use of such examples means that there is greater likelihood of pupils having some familiarity with one of the models. It may also happen that where these are contemporary, and in a modern idiom, the traits they demonstrate might be more attainable for a 13-year-old than the style of, say, George Orwell or Emily Brontë. If we extend this rationale to its logical conclusion, it may be possible too for Jonah to find good models in work from other pupils and other classes in the school, and to incorporate these in his examples.

The potential of the story openings

Here are the story openings used by Jonah as models for pupils' writing:

> Hale knew, before he had been in Brighton three hours, that they meant to murder him. With his inky fingers and his bitten nails, his manner cynical and nervous, anybody could tell he didn't belong – belong to the early summer sun, the cool Whitsun wind off the sea, the holiday crowd. (Graham Greene, *Brighton Rock*)

> It happened that green and crazy summer when Frankie was twelve years old. This was the summer when for a long time she had not been a member. She belonged to no club and was a member of nothing in the world. Frankie had become an unjoined person who hung around doorways, and she was afraid. (Carson McCullers, *The Member of the Wedding*)

> There was no possibility of taking a walk that day. We had been wandering, indeed, in the leafless shrubbery an hour in the morning; but since dinner (Mrs. Reed, when there was no company, dined early) the cold winter wind had brought with it clouds so sombre, and a rain so penetrating, that further out-door exercise was now out of the question. (Charlotte Brontë, *Jane Eyre*)

> It was a bright cold day in April, and the clocks were striking thirteen. Winston Smith, his chin nuzzled into his breast in an effort to escape the vile wind, slipped quickly through the glass doors of Victory Mansions, though not quickly enough to prevent a swirl of gritty dust from entering along with him. (George Orwell, *Nineteen Eighty-Four*)

We can see that across the collection, pupils have examples that hook readers with puzzles or questions, which swiftly suggest the unspoken backstory of protagonists, and which signal the nature of places and the relationships of characters to them. The examples also demonstrate the potential impact of a well-turned first sentence, in most of these short and clipped in style and without exception devoid of the figurative language many pupils may have been taught to regard as good writing. In *Brighton Rock*, the urgency of Hale's predicament is stressed by the subordinate clause, while we learn about him through carefully selected adjectives ('inky fingers' and 'bitten nails'). In the extract drawn from *The Member of the Wedding*, the protagonist is similarly introduced in the opening sentence, expressed in simple, even mundane vocabulary when we look at words in isolation. Against this backdrop, a phrase such as 'unjoined person' acquires significance because it is not an everyday idiom. Instead it is enigmatic, thought-provoking. Orwell's writing begins in similar style, the language of the first sentence sparse and largely monosyllabic. It is the strangeness of the detail that draws us, of the clock 'striking thirteen', though the impact of this on pupils cannot be guaranteed in a world of 24-hour clocks. Beyond that, the opening conveys to us the hostility of Winston's surroundings, the 'vile wind' and 'swirl of gritty dust' inescapable as he seeks shelter in Victory Mansions.

In these respects, then, Jonah has selected apt models that indicate features of the author's craft that might be replicated in pupil work. By framing them with that question about effectiveness, however, Jonah introduces a layer of difficulty that adds to the challenge presented by the texts themselves. The tutor offered these points for Jonah's consideration:

> There are different ways to exploit the story openings you provide as models. Often, these can build from quite simple prompts about pupils' preferences, making the most of the opportunity for contrast between the models. You can ask *Which do you like best? Why?* These questions are likely to provoke different responses to *Which is most effective?*, which frames response as academic and analytic from the outset, but which can be limited if pupils have not had opportunity to find personal or emotional resonance with the text first. Once a pupil has commented on their preferred text, you can ask them why it hooked them more successfully than another or in what respect it engaged them differently.

The priority for Jonah would thus be to stimulate comment about the texts and to avoid that lull he experienced by asking about 'effectiveness'. In his preparation, it would be useful for him to recognise what each text does especially well, and to be ready to emphasise this in his comments or through his questioning. *Brighton Rock*, for example, immediately prompts readers to wonder who pursues him, why they do so and how Hale came to know about it in the first place. He may wish to underline that the sentence prompts the reader to follow three lines of enquiry. It differs in its methods from *The Member of the Wedding*, where the use of 'that green and crazy summer' can set us thinking through the unusual juxtaposition of those adjectives. Is it the combination which gives them emphasis, and which in turn might lead us to wonder quite why it was crazy? Another approach might be to consider how the extracts quickly create cohesive worlds, for example how Jane Eyre builds the winter scene through 'leafless shrubbery', 'cold winter wind' and 'clouds so sombre'. Once attention is drawn to the cumulative technique there, how do details in *Nineteen Eighty-Four* combine to similar effect?

The potential of different models for writing

Earlier, Jonah recognised the possibilities of using texts more familiar to pupils. We can see how these can afford the same opportunities if we look at examples of story openings drawn from David Almond and Siobhan Dowd respectively, in each instance considering the first few lines rather than the full opening paragraph:

> My name is Erin Law. My friends are January Carr and Mouse Gullane. This is the story of what happened when we sailed away from Whitegates that Friday night. Some people will tell you that none of these things happened. They'll say they were just a dream that the three of us shared. But they did happen. We did meet Heaven Eyes on the Back Middens. We did dig the saint out of the mud. We did find Grampa's treasures and his secrets. We did see Grampa return to the river. And we did bring Heaven Eyes with us. She lives happily here among us ... (David Almond, *Heaven Eyes*)

> The place brought to mind a sinking ship. Wood creaked on the floor, across the pews, up in the gallery. Around the walls, a fierce March wind chased itself.
> The congregation launched into the Our Father as if every last soul was going down. Heaven. Bread. Trespass. Temptation. The words whisked past Shell's ears like rabbits vanishing into their holes. She tried wiggling her nose to make it slimmer ... (Siobhan Dowd, *A Swift Pure Cry*)

The extracts work differently and so suggest differing approaches for pupils. Almond's opening is very direct, starting with that grammatically simple sentence 'My name is Erin Law'. Erin continues from there to provide us with information concisely and directly so that we develop a sense of her voice, the people around her and her world. There are no instances of figurative language, no adjectives or adverbs. Proper nouns signal the distinctiveness of her realm, and perhaps it is the quirkiness of names like January and Mouse that intrigue, and place names like Back

Middens, which give the extract its distinctiveness. The passage offers up narrative details immediately, though the narrator seems to assume we may know these already, that we have familiarity with Heaven Eyes 'the saint', with Grampa and with the reasons for Erin's departure from Whitegates. What Erin communicates most emphatically is the veracity of her tale, asserting its legitimacy in the face of those who might suggest it was a dream. The opening is thus dense with information. At the same time it conveys a voice and something of Erin's urgency while providing hooks about characters, places and details as if incidentally, because we know these already, don't we? The passage serves as a good example for pupils of how to present information for readers while maintaining interest and even mystery. As Jonah tries to bridge reading and writing in his teaching, he could scaffold writing so that pupils list the proper nouns that are relevant to the world of their story, and ask them to identify a voice for their tale. If pupils can attribute to the voice feelings or a mood, they can begin to consider how the emotions of each narrator influence their expression.

If Jonah chooses to use the Dowd extract, other possibilities can be modelled, and the juxtaposition with another passage, whether from *Heaven Eyes* or another novel, makes the traits and effects of details easier to discuss by dint of the contrast. A question for pupils about who is telling each story would quickly point up the contrast between first person in Almond and the third person perspective here, though the last couple of sentences could give readers a strong sense of how Shell experiences and perceives things around her. One of those sentences also uses a simile to convey the power of certain words upon her, while the final sentence alights on the very specific movement of Shell's nose and her attributed intention. Both share with us something of her state of being, though she does not report it to us herself. The sense of person is thus created in a very different way to that of *Heaven Eyes*. Dowd evokes location differently too. What environment would pupils imagine if they heard only the opening sentence? Would it surprise them, then, to learn after hearing later sentences that this described a church? Is it easier for them to imagine and empathise with Shell's apparent isolation here than it is with Erin's circumstance in the first example? Once pupils can identify the extract that draws them in most successfully, they can begin to explain how it works. Again, the prompts for this may seem simple: *Which detail or sentence is most important for you? Which stays in your mind or pulls you in?* Ultimately, it is the distinctive affordance of the examples that is important, and the repertoire of approaches suggested across the selected models that pupils can then echo in their own work.

As another option, Jonah might find it useful to exploit published examples to prepare writing content for pupils so that they can concentrate on aspects of style. This would certainly be valid in instances where pupils are rehearsing the skills of writing a story opening before creating their own. Most of the published examples presented in this chapter intimate the completely formed narrative that follows and which may have been conceived before these were written: if you know the books they come from, you can usually see how they prefigure later details. If such a sense of the story in its entirety is sometimes a prerequisite for composing an effective opening, that is quite a challenge for pupils.

One response to this is to provide in the form of a list or bullet points the narrative information to be conveyed, leaving pupils to concentrate on the stylistic details. The challenge is then how to manipulate the information in order to hook a reader, not to generate it as well. In the case of *Heaven Eyes*, a list could include these items:

- You story will be told by Erin.
- Erin mentions two friends, January Carr and Mouse Gullane.
- Erin will explain a sequence of events, including leaving a place called Whitegates …

The items would follow this reductive formula, though one point could need emphasis:

- Erin thinks that some people won't believe her story, so she is keen to convince us that these things really happened.

Pupils can then experiment with preparing a story opening, compare their versions built around common content and reflect on the differing effects of their stylistic and sequencing decisions. Because these derive from common content, pupils' attention during peer-assessment will be more focused on the different choices of presentation they have made. Prompts for such work can be: *How did your partner's writing present information differently from yours? Did their work make Erin, her story or her world seem different? How does this affect you as you read? Does it create different thoughts or feelings?* The numerous opening passages that result also make manifest the matter of choice on the part of the author: here are perhaps twenty or thirty versions of the same story but crafted differently for varying effects upon their readers. The lesson could even conclude with shared attention to the source material, to Almond's writing, and consideration of the choices he made. Perhaps now Jonah could introduce that idea of 'effectiveness'. Can his pupils identify anything in their own writing that has a different effect from Almond's work, or which might be effective in a different way?

Conclusion

Jonah's lesson evidently had much merit and set out to challenge pupils with reference to literary models as a basis for their own work. He was also sensible to recognise that the effect of writing on readers is a central issue in this sort of activity. When presented as an abstraction called 'effectiveness', however, pupils can have great trouble considering it. This chapter has highlighted the importance of drawing on their already wide knowledge and experience as readers, and has suggested ways of eliciting it gently and in ways which support their developing confidence.

Jonah's instinct to provide examples as the basis for their own writing was also wise. If his pupils are to build on their existing capabilities as writers, they need some guidance of where to go next. The hard part in that process is to create a context in which the characteristics of literary models can be replicated and transformed for their own purposes. The strategy described here of using models drawn from the fiction they read for pleasure is intended to make the models seem less remote, their features more attainable.

Finally, the chapter has also hinted at scope for you during planning and shaping objectives to isolate the core skills for teaching as precisely as possible, for instance by separating the activities of generating ideas and content for a narrative from the processes of organising and articulating information for readers.

References

Almond, David (2000) *Heaven Eyes*. London: Hodder Children's Books.

AQA (2012) *Higher Tier June 2012 English Literature 47101H Unit 1 Exploring modern texts Tuesday 22 May 2012*. Manchester: AQA.

Assessment Reform Group (2002) *Assessment for Learning: 10 Principles*. University of Cambridge School of Education, Assessment Reform Group.

Assessment Reform Group (2005) *Assessment for Learning: Beyond the Black Box. Principles of Assessment for Learning*. University of Cambridge School of Education, Assessment Reform Group, pp. 77–96.

Bernstein, Basil (1973) *Class, Codes and Control*. St Albans: Paladin.

Black, Paul and Wiliam, Dylan (1990) *Inside the Black Box*. London: GL Assessment.

Black, Paul, Harrison, Christine, Lee, Clare, Marshall, Bethan and Wiliam, Dylan (1990) *Working Inside The Black Box: Assessment for Learning in the Classroom*. London: GL Assessment.

Bloom, Benjamin (ed.) (1979) *Taxonomy of Educational Objectives: Handbook 1, Cognitive Domain*. London: Longman Group.

Brontë, Charlotte (1847) *Jane Eyre*. London: Penguin.

DfE (2013) *English Programmes of Study: Key Stage 3 (National Curriculum in England)*. Reference: DFE-00184-2013.

Dowd, Siobhan (2007) *A Swift Pure Cry*. London: Random House.

Greene, Graham (1938) *Brighton Rock*. London: Penguin.

Hawe, Eleanor M. and Dixon, Helen R. (2014) 'Building students' evaluative and productive expertise in the writing classroom', *Assessing Writing*, 19 (January): 66–79.

Krathwohl, David, Bloom, Benjamin and Masia, Bertram (1971) *Taxonomy of Educational Objectives: Handbook 2, Affective Domain*. London: Longman Group.

McCullers, Carson (1946) *The Member of the Wedding*. London: Penguin.

Myhill, Debra (2005) 'Ways of knowing: writing with grammar in mind', *English Teaching: Practice and Critique*, 4 (3): 77–96.

National Literacy Trust (2013) *Literacy Guide for Schools 2013–14*. Online at: http://www.literacytrust.org.uk/our_network/guide.

Orwell, George (1949/1987) *Nineteen Eighty-Four*. London: Penguin.

Samuels, Diane (2008) *Kindertransport*. London: Nick Hern Books.

Wray, David, Medwell, Jane, Fox, Richard and Poulson, Louise (2000) 'The teaching practices of effective teachers of literacy', *Educational Review*, 52 (1): 75–84.

Wyse, Dominic (2004) 'Grammar for writing? A critical review of empirical evidence', *British Journal of Educational Studies*, 49 (4): 411–27.

CHAPTER 5

TEACHING ABOUT LANGUAGE

Objectives of this chapter:

- To consider aspects of the English curriculum related to language study, which are closer to linguistics than literary study
- To identify the challenges and potential of analysing instances of language as transcripts
- To look at the specialist vocabulary relevant to language analysis and identify generalisable strategies for introducing pupils to specialist vocabulary across all areas of English

Introduction

If the curriculum for English encompassed only literature, the discipline might have a different name. It could be 'Literary Studies' or 'Language Arts' as it is some territories. That the subject is called English points to an emphasis on language too, though studying English in school here does not usually work to the same principles as other language-based disciplines such as French, Japanese or Spanish when they are studied as additional languages. Where the English of the National Curriculum has statutory force it represents the national language (though not without challenge in Wales), and as such it is entwined with national identity. It can be about 'being English' as well as about having the capacity to use the English language confidently and with fluency.

Any curriculum is the outcome of choice and design, whether created in a school or at the level of national government. The secondary phase English National Curriculum (DfE, 2013, 2014) embodies attitudes and beliefs about the English language and the nation's literature. Some of these are overt, others are tacit (in what is omitted, for instance); all can influence how pupils think about language and themselves. If pupils become conscious of failure in the subject, or come to feel that the curriculum does not reflect the world as they experience it, they can feel it excludes them. The English curriculum thus has great power to confer and confirm identities and values, but also to diminish any others that it does not include or represent (see the Ajegbo Review (DfCS, 2007) for further discussion).

While most people can recall being directed in 'proper' or Standard use of English at school, there will be many who have not had chance to explore the attitudes and beliefs surrounding language use. This will depend on when they were at school and whether or not the curriculum they followed treated language as a discrete object of study beyond a prescribed model of grammar. The history of the English curriculum, especially its recent past, shows that the model of language study adopted for schools fluctuates. Sometimes the prescriptive model dominates, while other periods permit some descriptive and exploratory treatment of language (see Crystal, 2004: 523–34 for discussion). If you read the government report on literacy and English published in the 1970s entitled *A Language for Life* (DES, 1975), you will be able to trace an interest in language approached from the perspective of sociolinguistics. The influence of the London School, of the likes of James Britton and Douglas Barnes (see Barnes et al., 1969), runs through it. It allows for studying language in context, with respect to relationships of power and social change. Everyday language is an object fit for study – is essential to study – if young people are to understand the world around them. Some commentators view the current curriculum (DfE, 2013) as representative of a prescriptive model, though the legacy of earlier curriculum detail remains apparent in continued units focused on spoken language study at GCSE (see, for example, AQA, 2014). Here is space to hold a descriptive orientation, for pupils to look at how language works, to consider varying perspectives and to reflect on its links with power, influence and representation.

As a beginning teacher you will need to be aware of the different ways language can be studied. It may be that you will not find an immediate opportunity to use approaches that reflect each of these models, but you can anticipate that across your career you will need to in response to curriculum changes that will probably embody different models at different times. This chapter describes Lizzy's work around an instance of spoken language in a television interview and the demands such teaching makes of her. She works with both a video recording of the interview and a transcript on the page. The process tests her nascent teaching skills and requires a pedagogy that looks very different from what she does elsewhere in her placement teaching.

Lizzy's lesson design

Lizzy is working with a Year 10 class of mixed ability, guiding them towards a GCSE assessment focused on the study of spoken language. Lizzy is established in a second placement, in the final third of her course. She has worked with the class for some time, and has led them through two other units already. She experiences no overt difficulties of classroom management with the group and has built a strong rapport with the pupils.

The objectives Lizzy proposes for the lesson are as follows:

1. For pupils to know the features of a transcript.
2. For pupils to understand how transcripts represent spoken language in print.
3. For pupils to analyse a transcript using specialised vocabulary.

Resources for the lesson

The key resources for the lesson are a video extract showing the television interview and a transcript of the exchange shown on the video.

The texts used here come from the resource *Investigating Spoken Language* published by the English and Media Centre. The transcript matches video footage of an interview on the BBC's evening magazine programme, *The One Show*. The interviewing roles are held here by Adrian Chiles and Christine Bleakley with Chris Evans as a guest. The interview is studio-based, with Chris Evans apparently just arriving, in some hurry, as a motorbike passenger. His journey becomes the first topic in the exchange, then his recently published autobiography.

The video extract is well selected by Lizzy. It shows an exchange that typifies the interview format of the show and daily television programming generally, and hence it is a 'found object' of spoken language study needing no contrivance for the purposes of teaching. At the same time it has distinctive interest as an object for spoken language study because of the status of the participants. Though Evans is the interviewee, he has wide experience of interviewing himself, and so the usual balance of power in interviewing situations is altered. In retrospect there is also added frisson given the subsequent media spat between Chiles and Evans that resulted from Evans' appointment as anchorman to the Friday edition of the programme and the subsequent departure of Chiles to ITV.

The exchange provides scope to apply methods of analysis that are distinctive to this domain of the subject. In particular, participants refer to objects in the immediate setting. These references make sense to viewers, but are not transparent in a transcript. In this example, Evans draws attention to the direction of Chiles' gaze, suggesting he is looking for a copy of the autobiography. Where Lizzy's objective is to help pupils understand the relationship between a transcript and spoken language, an instance like this has a useful degree of obviousness that can help pupils understand that spoken language exchanges between participants can reflect a shared context that may not be apparent to others and which may not be articulated in explicit terms in talk. It is only through seeing the video here that pupils could know exactly what was happening. Selecting instances like these, which make features of transcripts and phenomena of spoken language very clear, can be important to establishing pupils' understanding before they attempt to discuss more subtle instances. The impact of teaching here, then, is closely tied to the teacher's judgement in how to use resources and where to place emphasis.

The transcript is the resource that is most unfamiliar and novel to pupils. They have not worked with this format before. Their nearest reference point is the format of play script, which they will have encountered frequently since primary school. This particular transcript is presented in Times New Roman font, around size point 12, with approximately single line spacing. The transcript is limited to one side of A4 paper so that pupils can see it in its entirety. The names of participants are abbreviated to the initials AC (Adrian Chiles), CB (Christine Bleakley) and CE (Chris Evans).

Teaching the lesson

Lizzy's lesson design is one of good structure, having phases and activities that link with each of the objectives. Lizzy today manages the classroom very well and is able to teach to her lesson plan in the sequence intended. After introducing the learning objectives, Lizzy shows pupils the video extract. Their viewing is informed by a prompt: to identify features of spoken language apparent in the exchange. At this point pupils do not have access to the transcript and the brief plenary feedback comprises general observations shared by pupils selected by Lizzy. These activities comprise the first ten minutes of the lesson.

In the next phase, Lizzy shares the transcript in hard copy with pupils. Lizzy anticipates the novelty of the transcript for pupils and directs them to consider what aspects of the format seem unfamiliar. She gives pupils three minutes to highlight or circle any unusual features and then gives them a further three minutes to share their initial thoughts with their neighbour. Lizzy rounds off the phase by eliciting contributions from pupils, taking opportunity to introduce specialised vocabulary where it corresponds with pupils' 'common-sense' observations. Where pupils note the use of 'well' and 'er', for example, Lizzy introduces the term 'filler'.

The next part of the lesson entails pupils working with their copy of the transcript independently and over a longer period. This activity relates to the second objective, understanding how spoken language is reflected in print. Over the opening five minutes pupils annotate the transcript individually, seeking details that they believe only occur in spoken language. Lizzy encourages pupils to use the terminology identified in the previous phase where appropriate, but also urges pupils not to get too bound up in applying the specialist vocabulary: 'The important thing is to find details that show you this is speech.' Once again, the individual work is followed by pair work, then group work (one pair joining another), leading to plenary discussion and continued shared annotation. Lizzy draws contributions from groups, annotating a copy of the transcript projected for the whole class through the use of a visualiser. As she writes, Lizzy adds the specialist vocabulary if pupils haven't used it. The activity of pupils extends across 20 minutes, and the collective guided annotation takes the remainder of the lesson.

Lizzy reflects on the lesson

Lizzy led the class in activities that related to her objectives and used some helpful strategies to gauge pupils' developing understanding. The device of moving from individual thinking time to paired whole-class discussion gave pupils the chance to refine their ideas and contributed to the quality of pupils' comments in the latter part of the lesson.

Reflecting on her lesson, Lizzy reviewed pupils' progress in relation to her stated learning objectives. She felt that she gave pupils time to consider the features of a transcript but that she missed the opportunity to specify relevant features with precision. Though pupils could remark on aspects of the transcript, she felt they did not explain these sufficiently to show they understood what makes a transcript distinct from an ostensibly similar form such as a play script. She also commented, 'I'm not sure how well they will recall the features as we didn't record them in a systematic way.' Lizzy recognised similar scope for refinement around the objective 'to understand how transcripts represent spoken language in print': 'There's an irony that in aiming to help them appreciate features of spoken language, we spent the majority of the lesson looking at language in printed form. I think I would have got closer to *how* transcripts represent speech if I'd spent a little longer on the video in the first place.' Lizzy recognised that she had some success in introducing specialised vocabulary, and her tutor stressed the value of her approach in introducing the terms gradually as their relevance became apparent. It seemed that pupils were not intimidated by the new vocabulary and that most proved able to use some of it in their annotation. Lizzy elaborated the point to observe that though some used it, she didn't have a good sense of which terms everyone used and still less which ones they understood. She recalled a point in the final plenary phase where she elaborated on a pupil's identification of turns in conversation that worked together, introducing the term 'adjacency pair' (see Hutchby and Wooffitt, 1998). She sensed most pupils were a little put off by the term and evidently had not used it themselves.

Using a transcript with a class

Transcripts can be an excellent resource as they supply a focal point for discussion by pupils and support their close analysis of spoken language texts where otherwise information is ephemeral and difficult to recall. In this lesson Lizzy had scope to exploit her transcript further to aid pupils' engagement with features that are particular to spoken language. In the lesson her pupils seemed generally at ease with this new format, perhaps because the way they approached it (and were led to approach it) was very similar to what they were used to in literary analysis. In this respect, however, the apparent ease of the lesson and high levels of pupil engagement do not necessarily correlate with depth of learning.

There are a couple of things Lizzy could try prior to the page-based analysis, to help pupils keep in mind the fact that the transcript is a representation of spoken language, and not the phenomenon itself. First, Lizzy can exploit the video extract further. If time permits she can show it twice. Because this lesson is about the analysis of spoken language, pupils' initial and relatively unmediated reactions to an instance of spoken language are likely to be helpful as a basis for analysis. The first viewing, then, can be presented in what might appear to be a relaxed manner, with prompts or questions that do not seem to be as incisive as one might expect of analysis. Nevertheless, asking pupils to describe the relationship of speakers and their attitudes to one another and to remark on some surface features of their talk provides an essential foundation. This phase may elicit perceptive comment from pupils that will be relevant to analysis even if it is not articulated in an overtly academic discourse. A second viewing might be framed with specific prompts, and if time is at a premium Lizzy may choose to focus on a short extract rather than the whole exchange. She may find turns that illustrate a variety of points she anticipates could be made, so the selection steers pupils to the material most likely to sustain depth of analysis.

Lizzy could also draw on strategies that are commonly used by teachers of Media Studies when using audio-visual texts. Often, teachers of media want to isolate a mode of communication where several are used simultaneously. With a film they can emphasise elements in the visual mode by removing the sound with a 'mute' facility. They can also concentrate on the sound of a text by blanking or covering the screen. Both techniques can lead to realisations that details in either mode can be overlooked when you encounter them working together, and can also help pupils' better understand the combined effect and impact of modes. Here Lizzy wants pupils to focus on spoken language, so it would help pupils simply to hear the exchange and not see the visual footage that matches the conversation. As a strategy to employ in other spoken language work, this has much potential. In some instances pupils could hear a conversation *before* seeing it in its full audio-visual presentation. The approach aids concentration on the verbal elements. With some texts, there may be interesting details of the context, other people or objects in the environment, that are significant to the progress of the conversation but which are not immediately clear to those simply listening. Examples like this can draw attention to the way in which spoken language is situated in a context, often of tangible physical surroundings, where referents are drawn on in conversation and understood by participants. In other cases, seeing the audio-visual text first will be essential because pupils need to see referents too to make progress in their comprehension. It is a matter of teacher judgement to decide which sequence best suits teaching purposes, and whether or not the manipulation of the text can draw attention to any of its salient features of language.

A further very simple technique is to have pupils work with a transcript verbally before they take pens to it by way of annotation. In groups or across a class, the teacher can ask them to read the transcript rather as they would a play script. This task means they should respond to the printed detail, not only the words but also whatever orthography matches the transcription conventions relevant to this piece. If the conventions used include capitalising words that require emphasis or an increase in volume, they can try to reflect that in their own utterances. This means that as they read through the transcript, what on the face of it appears a functional though fun means of 'getting through' the focus text also becomes the means to engage pupils in the transcription conventions. In being alert to these, and by following the transcript more broadly, pupils experience the exchange as conversation themselves. At a very simple level it may help them note changes in turn, but it can also draw their attention to puzzling aspects of an exchange that may not be fully explained by the detail of a transcript where it is encountered without audio accompaniment. In this regard, reading aloud is a process of familiarisation, of living the detail of the exchange and getting to know it. Again, the process helps emphasise features of the exchange which may be followed up in more conventionally detached analysis.

A final possibility is perhaps the most active of all: asking pupils to become authors of a transcript themselves. One version of this strategy entails asking pupils to work from an extract of the video which spans several turns. Ideally the selected extract will feature distinctive aspects of spoken language very prominently, for instance clearly variable intonation and emphasis, utterances and paralinguistic communication, and overlapping. The transcription exercise can be framed as problem-solving, the teacher asking pupils to capture in their transcripts as much information as possible about the spoken language of the exchange. A likely starting point for pupils would be to get the words down first, more akin to a play script, so a teacher could anticipate this as a first stage and then suggest to pupils some of the other elements. Alternatively, the teacher might find it more efficient to present pupils with the words that are used and then ask them to decide how they want to indicate the other elements of spoken communication. The underlying aim is to make pupils alert to the dimensions of spoken language that are not generally presented in print. In being asked to formulate their own means of conveying these dimensions, they are led to engage with the function of a transcript directly.

A variation on this approach would be to work with established conventions, providing pupils with a transcript for the opening turns in an exchange together with a glossary consistent with recognised and established orthography. First, viewing the related video extract two or three times over can stimulate discussion about its relationship with the transcribed version and consolidate pupils' understanding of the transcription conventions. The teacher can then task pupils with completing the transcription for the next few turns. As with the previous approach this can be started from scratch or built around words already provided so that focus is maintained on the paralinguistic resources of spoken language. This latter focus compels pupils to use the transcription conventions with great care and supports their close attention to the same symbols and their significance when they come to analyse other transcripts in the same vein. It may be that the teacher takes this approach only with a very short extract and then provides a full published transcript for pupils shortly after. In this case, pupils' transcription activity is a means to support the acuity of their later analysis and a more involving option than the teacher explaining the glossary to the class in a lecture-style. If Lizzy were to take this approach and monitor pupils' use of the conventions, she would have the means to gauge their understanding of them and could improve the impact of her teaching with respect to her second objective, 'to understand how transcripts represent spoken language in print'. The exercise would also provide some response to her reservation about focusing too much on a printed text, affording pupils' sustained and deep engagement with the spoken language text instead.

Exploiting transcripts fully

The transcript Lizzy used was set out well in a clear font, though in the lesson it was not presented alongside an accompanying glossary of conventions. It would assist pupils to have access to a glossary, and to have the turns in the exchange numbered for ease of reference. This will have particular benefits during whole-class discussion, where it becomes important for pupils to refer to details in the transcript precisely so that others can locate the same items with ease. Numbering the turns also makes it easier for the teacher to record details arising from pupils' remarks swiftly. The teacher can write the isolated turn by number on the board, with a brief note summarising pupils' observations, or record connected turns where pupils see links between these (for example, linked pairs such as question and answer, often called 'adjacency pairs').

Using a transcription glossary

One resource Lizzy omitted to provide for her pupils was a glossary. A glossary can be exploited in many different ways, though perhaps the most essential aspect of introducing a glossary is to stress the nature of details in the transcript. In some transcription conventions, details such as commas or full stops indicate pauses of differing lengths rather than signal the boundaries of a syntactic unit, though sometimes those different functions coincide. Pupils will need to know these distinctions if they are to read a transcript and remark on it with the necessary subtlety. They will also need to have the formatting explained. In this material based on *The One Show*, turns that overlap are indicated through alignment so that an open square bracket marks the beginning of the overlap in each contribution:

CB: you've come straight from there, to here, on a motorbike. [Just for us
CE: [Well,   we
      did, I did the last 20 minutes, on the back of the motorbike.

It may also be apt to indicate to pupils that the glossary and conventions they use are just one approach of many possible alternatives. One need not dwell too much on showing other forms of transcription, but quickly displaying two or three where the formatting clearly looks different would press the point. A transcript rendered via Conversation Analysis (see Hutchby and Wooffitt, 1998) will look rather more alien than a discourse analysis transcript (see Hammersley, 2003), for example, given the close attention to aspects of intonation and the precise duration of silences and pauses. The distinction may not be the focus of stated learning objectives, but making the various options apparent combats a potential misconception that transcription takes only one form. Indeed, the suggestion that these different models of language study exist foreshadows A-level English Language work and manifests an open-minded ethos to diverse and descriptive models rather than fixed, prescriptive perspectives.

Helping pupils to use specialist vocabulary

During Lizzy's lesson, the specialised metalanguage for analysing talk was introduced with some spontaneity, largely as and when pupils described phenomena in the transcript that correlated with recognised terms. In most cases Lizzy explained these orally in relation to their examples, also using the specialist vocabulary in her annotations on the transcript visible as a model to the whole class. Lizzy's assertion that she could not really say who used the terms or the extent to which they understood them is a fair one. If we return to the detail she raised concerning an 'adjacency pair', what steps might Lizzy take in future to increase the likelihood of pupils using and understanding the term? Whatever principles she uses to introduce this term can be used with other terminology too, and not just here but in other topic areas of English. The task of learning specialist jargon is relevant to literary study, drama study and media in the curriculum, and can also be considered relative to what EAL specialists call 'cognitive academic language proficiency' (Cummins, 2000). Pupils may understand specialised concepts and have the capacity to express them in everyday language but can struggle to use the correct academic vocabulary associated with a subject discipline. In EAL pedagogy, this means stepping beyond 'basic interpersonal communication' and using the subject-specific discourse with accuracy and fluency. In effect this is about giving pupils access to a discourse, and has implications for their access to any unfamiliar discourse they might encounter across school (for instance, in various subjects) or in the world beyond, whether in the context of employment (a professional discourse) or for personal housekeeping (the language of contracts, insurance or banking).

In conversation with Lizzy, her tutor presents this suite of strategies to support more deliberate and focused attention on the key terms. She could choose any one of these according to her purpose, or use and adapt them in combination:

1. Adopt an initially didactic approach, introducing terminology by definition and example.
2. Provide the pupils with a term and its explanation, and ask pupils to identify an instance of the phenomenon in a text.
3. Ask pupils to identify an instance of the phenomenon from their own experience or immediate context.
4. Ask pupils to create an illustrative example that typifies the term.
5. Provide pupils with a range of textual examples (such as four or five instances), some of which demonstrate the phenomenon and some of which do not. Pupils can pick out the examples that provide a match for the term. Further, they can also be asked to explain how and why these match and how they differ from mismatched examples.
6. Present several instances of the phenomenon and ask pupils to explain what they have in common, and only afterwards introduce

the specialist term. The teacher can then ask pupils to write a definition based on the verbalisations of the phenomenon they have just shared.

7. Present several different phenomena in the text and several different terms, asking pupils to match them correctly.
8. Explain and discuss the phenomenon orally. Present pupils with three definitions that are similar but only one of which is correct. Ask pupils to select the one that is exactly right and explain why.
9. Highlight a number of phenomena (for example, three examples) and ask pupils to apply the correct term to each, and perhaps a definition for each too.
10. Present two texts that share the same phenomenon, ask pupils to find the common feature and name it by applying the correct term.

All but the first also act as assessments of pupils' ability to recognise the phenomenon and link it to the correct term, with some suggestions offering more subtle means of gauging understanding. Suggestions 6 and 7 include a written element. Though pupils' written work can indicate pupils' understanding, it is not the only means to assess it. A pupil may very well understand what an adjacency pair is but could still have difficulty explaining it in their own writing. Though Lizzy may wish to help pupils in their capacity to define it, she may find that the ability to apply the term correctly is the most important skill for pupils in their formally assessed responses.

Conclusion

In addition to emphasising the issue of linguistic jargon as a potential barrier to pupils' learning unless introduced with care, this chapter has described strategies that could help Lizzy exploit her pupils' tacit knowledge of language. Some of this can be activated through creative activity such as designing their own transcription method for everyday texts. This approach is also a form of problem-solving, as if they were for the first time inventing means to convey the features of spoken language on the page.

Other strategies focus on how to isolate spoken language, for instance by removing the accompanying video when considering spoken language in audio-visual texts. Much of this is motivated by a need to keep pupils' attention on the aural mode of communication, and to help them appreciate how it functions distinctively and discretely, as well as understanding how it works alongside other modes such as gesture, temporally across a sequence, or with reference to the immediate environment and participants. You may find that just like Lizzy, you find that it is only through teaching such processes that you develop your judgement about how to emphasise these aspects, and recognise that something as simple as the distribution of time and discussion spent on both the instance of spoken language (in an audio recording or film) and then on the transcript can have quite an impact on how successfully pupils analyse the various elements.

References

AQA (2014) *GCSE Specification: English Language 4705*. Manchester: AQA.

Barnes, Douglas, Britton, James, Rosen, Harold and LATE (1969) *Language, the Learner and the School*. Harmondsworth: Penguin.

Clark, Christina and De Zoysa, Sarah (2011) *Mapping the Interrelationships of Reading Enjoyment, Attitudes, Behaviour and Attainment: An Exploratory Investigation*. London: National Literacy Trust.

Crystal, David (2004) *The Stories of English*. London: Allen Lane.

Cummins, Jim (2000) *Language, Power and Pedagogy: Bilingual Children in the Crossfire*. Clevedon: Multilingual Matters.

DES (1975) *A Language for Life* (Bullock Report). London: HMSO.

DfCS (2007) *The Diversity and Curriculum Review*. Nottingham: DfCS.

DfE (2013) *English Programmes of Study: Key Stage 3 (National Curriculum in England)*. Reference: DFE-00184-2013.

DfE (2014) *English Programmes of Study: Key Stage 4 (National Curriculum in England)*. Reference: DFE-00497-2014.

Halliday, Michael A. K. (1985) *An Introduction to Functional Grammar*. London: Edward Arnold.

Hammersley, Martin (2003) 'Conversation analysis and discourse analysis: methods or paradigms?', *Discourse and Society*, 14: 751–77.

Hutchby, Ian and Wooffitt, Robin (1998) *Conversation Analysis*. Cambridge: Polity Press.

CHAPTER 6

TEACHING POINTS OF GRAMMAR

Objectives of this chapter:

- To provide a summary of the current requirements for the teaching of grammar, including the context in the primary phase prior to secondary phase study
- To introduce different perspectives on what constitutes effective grammar teaching
- To suggest the use of research evidence to inform practice
- To illustrate the application of research to lesson design, with examples based on teaching apostrophe use

---

Introduction

In May 2013 primary school pupil Rebecca Lee wrote to the Secretary of State for Education at that time, Michael Gove, to draw his attention to errors of spelling and punctuation in the test she had just completed:

Dear Mr Gove,

I am writing to inform you of a number of mistakes that occurred in the spelling test that I, as a Year 6 pupil, did today.

In this assessment paper there were three punctuation errors in the sentences.

Having discussed this as a class, we think that one of these mistakes is perhaps debatable.

However, we are unanimously agreed about the other two errors.

This means that over 10% of the questions contained an error.

I understand that you are very keen for us all to learn our complex sentences and use of accurate punctuation.

I believe that your department should also use the correct punctuation in all the SATS tasks.

I am very surprised that you have allowed these mistakes to occur.

As the Secretary of State for Education you are responsible for these tests and your department should be setting us a better example.

I would like to hear what you have to say about this and also whether you will perhaps admit that punctuation is often a matter of judgement, with not necessarily a single right answer.

Yours sincerely,

Rebecca Lee

(The Mirror, 2013)

Gove (2010) was not unusual in making spelling and grammar prominent in his speeches about improving standards in education. Both areas were frequently invoked by Labour and subject to attention in the curricular reforms of their post-millennium governments (for an example, see David Blunkett's foreword to Labour's curriculum (DfEE, 1999)). Debates about spelling and grammar have persisted since the advent of English as a school discipline, usually with the slant that standards are declining, an inexorable trend of diminishing literacy skills in young people. A remark made by representatives of Boots the Chemists, that 'most young people are simply ill-prepared for the demands of the work place' could be as true today as it was in 1917. That the debates persist, and that there is a continuing perception of a spelling and grammar problem, suggests that there is no consensus, no resolution about how best to teach them. As Rebecca's alertness suggests, the generalisation that poor standards are endemic in young people is problematic. A survey of web use by IBM found that '40 per cent of those aged 18–24 are influenced [as in put off] by poor spelling and grammar compared with 35 per cent on average across all age categories' (*The Telegraph*, 2012), and suggested they were more discerning than their elders in using 'traditional markers of quality' to evaluate the merit of web sources. Rebecca's letter describes current testing arrangements that concentrate on print-based literacy in a print-based format. Maybe the assessment regime fails to gauge the skills that young people draw on in their web use. This is just one example of a tension, if not contradiction, in received wisdom about literacy standards.

In this uncertain context, what other difficulties do beginning teachers in the secondary phase experience around aspects of grammar teaching, what do they need to consider, and what approaches might they take?

Context for spelling and grammar – requirements

All phases of education in mainstream school have faced change in frameworks for spelling and grammar teaching since 2010. The history of the curriculum across the last twenty years suggests that the frequency of change is unlikely to abate. One difficulty for teachers in the 11–18 phase is how to understand what their pupils can do with respect to spelling and grammar when they arrive in secondary school. This can be difficult to grasp when curricular detail in those earlier key stages changes so frequently. Just as important for the secondary teacher is an awareness of how their pupils came to acquire those skills and what formulated their *understanding* of grammar and spelling. What terminology did pupils learn and use to describe what happens in the English language? What labels did they use, what metalanguage, to describe the components of communication? What was emphasised and when, in what sequence: what curricular model of progression in language, grammar and spelling did they follow? All of these things will have a bearing on pupils' use of language in the secondary classroom, their ability to talk about and reflect upon language use and perhaps their values (tacit or otherwise) about what is important when evaluating language. These factors may also shape their self-esteem (do they believe they are 'good spellers'?) and even their conception of what constitutes English as a subject. It is not uncommon for young people to view it unfavourably as they bring to this secondary phase discipline their preconceptions of literacy, which can often be negative (for example, low enjoyment of reading in the primary phase), though the trend appears to have been arrested (National Literacy Trust, 2014). How should a secondary teacher of English take account of those previous influences in their own teaching of grammar and spelling?

English specialists in the 11–18 phase are likely to have most interest in the official requirements that affect them and their pupils directly, such as revisions to the GCSE specifications for English and to a lesser degree English Literature. Nevertheless, the changes at primary level can also have a significant impact. In March 2012 the union of head teachers voted to boycott the government's introduction of a compulsory test of 11-year-olds' spelling, grammar and punctuation, planned to start in 2015 (*The Independent*, 2012). The proposed tests would generate data likely to affect the experience of secondary teachers of English on a daily basis. In a period where they are constantly asked to ensure pupils make 'expected progress' against national benchmarks, they can be certain that their own performance will be measured according to their own capacity to ensure pupils' progress upon these tests for pupils aged 11, and hence at the end of Key Stage 2.

The current curricular requirements before pupils reach the secondary phase are these. In Key Stage 1, the curriculum emphasises phonics as a system to support reading (decoding) and writing (encoding). This entails pupils having explicit teaching in the phonics system of the English language, and learning about the relationship between sounds (or rather units of sound, phonemes) and their corresponding graphic representation by single letters or combinations of letters ('c', 'k' and 'ck' are available graphemes for the hard 'c' sound in English). Since early 2014 all pupils undergo 'phonics screening', a test in which they must sound out and verbalise (blend) 40 words presented to them in print. Some of these are 'pseudo words', vocabulary constructed specially for the purposes of the test.

At Key Stage 2, most pupils must complete a test comprised of two papers. The first is based on short-answer questions assessing grammar, punctuation and vocabulary. Some have a selective aspect (for example, multiple choice questions), while others require short open responses of words, phrases or sentences. The second paper assesses spelling. A test administrator reads a number of sentences aloud, in each omitting a word. Pupils must write down an appropriate word to fill the gap. These arrangements apply to pupils working between levels 3 and 5 in this key stage, and are supplemented by a three-part test for pupils working at level 6 or above. Here, an extended task assesses children's grammar, punctuation and vocabulary through a short piece of writing.

The rationale for the tests is explained to parents thus, signalling the relevance of test results to transition to secondary school:

> … we want to make sure that when children leave primary school they are confident in grammar, punctuation and spelling. The test will ensure that primary schools place a stronger focus on the teaching of these skills than in previous years …

The test results will provide teachers with useful information about a child's progress in each of the key areas. Most children will move to a secondary school the following term, and their new English teachers can use this information to focus their lessons on areas of need.

Another Key Stage 2 document English teachers may find useful for planning is the Department for Education's 'Glossary of Terms' (DfE, 2013). Official expectation is that these terms will be used when pupils are asked to label and discuss language. Many of the terms will be predictable and already widely addressed in secondary school (for example, adjective, conjunction and subject), though others may be novel and rarely introduced deliberately. These include *appropriacy, demarcation* and *fronted adverbial*. The entry for the last item provides this definition:

> An adverbial is any word, phrase or clause that functions like an adverb … An adverbial can be placed at the beginning, middle or end of a clause, e.g.:
>
> - At the railway station, I waited for my train to Manchester.
> - I waited at the railway station for my train to Manchester.
> - I waited for my train to Manchester at the railway station.

Since an adverbial's usual position is at the end of a sentence, it is described as 'fronted' when at the front and 'embedded' when it is in the middle.

Though these lists are non-statutory, the DfE 'programmes of study' documentation asserts 'it is important that pupils learn the correct grammatical terms in English and that these terms are integrated within teaching' (DfE, 2013). Secondary teachers of English will need to be aware of the glossary and the extent to which its terms, definitions and examples are used in Key Stage 2 teaching if they are to help their pupils make links with their prior experience of language study and make progress on those foundations.

The same is true of spelling, for which the KS2 curriculum prescribes a list of words that all pupils should know and write correctly. The list for Years 5 and 6 includes words often recognised as problematic, such as 'accommodate' and 'achieve', but also words we might not anticipate requiring overt attention such as 'cemetery', 'nuisance' and 'yacht'. It is an additional statutory requirement in these year groups to formally teach selected suffixes, such as 'endings which sound like /ʃəs/ spelt -cious or -tious', and to address possible confusion around homophones (words that sound the same but which have different spelling) such as 'affect' and 'effect'. Secondary teachers will not automatically assume that just because pupils have spent time looking at these words and patterns they will use them correctly in their writing, but knowing which items have statutory force prior to secondary school will help them plan for progress and to make apt and early interventions where pupils seem insecure in these details. It also helps to know that pupils should since Year 2 have had familiarity with the apostrophe of contraction, though consistently accurate use by pupils may be unlikely.

The 'grammar and vocabulary' programme of study for Key Stage 3 is brief (DfE, 2013). It expects that pupils will be taught to 'consolidate and build on their knowledge of grammar and vocabulary through extending and applying the grammatical knowledge' set out in the earlier key stages. Progression comes through a change in emphasis, with pupils now required to reflect on the 'effectiveness and impact of the grammatical features of the texts' they read and in those they compose themselves. When they describe language they should make 'precise and confident use of linguistic and literary terminology'. In general, they should use 'standard English confidently in their own writing'.

Since 2012, spelling, punctuation and grammar (often abbreviated to SPaG) have had renewed attention at GCSE in English and English Literature examinations, but also in Geography, History and Religious Studies where pupils are similarly required to write answers in extended prose. In each of those subjects, pupils have 5 per cent of their examination marks allocated to an assessment of spelling, punctuation and grammar. In English, the spelling of pupils is assessed separately from other features of their writing described in more holistic criteria (Ofqual, 2014).

Research evidence about teaching spelling and grammar

While the curriculum has changed swiftly and with some degree of assertiveness, research findings on the most effective ways to teach spelling and grammar are at variance and do not convey the same certainty that there is a single correct approach. Most surveys qualify their findings with care. The curriculum details outlined above suggest spelling and grammar can be learned through explicit and discrete teaching. While this approach has support in some research data, so does grammar teaching in context, an approach that involves teaching spelling and grammar in close alignment with processes of writing rather than as isolated topics.

In 2004 a systematic review of the research evidence concerning grammar teaching set out to examine what the authors described as the 'polarised' views of its merits, 'with a belief among some teachers, newspaper editors and members of the public, that such teaching is effective, and among others that it is ineffective' (Andrews et al., 2004). The first part of the study focused on the links between teaching about syntax and the accuracy and quality of pupils' written composition. It found that of the studies available, the three of highest quality presented contradictory conclusions. One found 'that traditional or transformational syntax teaching had virtually no influence on the language growth of typical secondary school students'. A second made the tentative suggestion 'that a generative grammar approach does make a difference to syntactic quality and to the control of malformed sentences'. A third study concentrating on 'elementary school African-American pupils' concluded that 'mastery of written forms of standard English is improved by using strategies for labelling and identifying grammatical features and by practising these forms and receiving teacher feedback'.

The second strand of the review looked at the merits of teaching about 'sentence combining'. The studies consulted suggested that this strategy was 'an effective means of improving the syntactic maturity of students in written English between the ages of 5 and 16'. The impact of such teaching was apparently most evident in 'immediate post-test effects … with some tempering of the effect in delayed post-tests'. The authors called for the revision of National Curriculum guidance to acknowledge sentence combining as an effective method.

Since then, the study *Grammar for Writing?* (see Jones et al., 2013) has recommended an embedded approach to the teaching of grammar within the context of writing. This found 'a statistically significant beneficial effect on students' writing attainment', but also recognised the importance of teachers' own 'grammatical and metalinguistic subject knowledge' and its influence on the effectiveness of teaching. Follow-up work concluding in 2014 set out to develop training and teaching materials based on research-based interventions, with the overarching aim of better understanding 'how the teaching of grammar might influence students' metalinguistic understanding, ability to analyse texts and ability to make conscious design choices in their writing'.

A lesson in grammar: Barney teaches apostrophes

Barney teaches a lesson to a Year 9 class which includes the return of marked written work. Pupils completed a non-fiction piece of writing with the purposes to inform and persuade. While marking, Barney noticed that some pupils used apostrophes inaccurately in their compositions. He had noted similar patterns across other pieces he had taken in from the class previously. Today's lesson has learning objectives focused on further non-fiction writing, with a different purpose. However, Barney has chosen to devote some time to apostrophe use in the lesson, first returning work to pupils, and then highlighting the issues around apostrophe use through general and mostly positive oral feedback. The section of the lesson devoted to activity around the apostrophe is billed as a 'starter' phase of around ten minutes, prior to the main body of the lesson focused on writing to argue and explain.

Barney asks his pupils to look closely at their work and to see where he has highlighted apostrophe use. Items highlighted in green confirm for pupils that they have used apostrophes correctly. Items in yellow show pupils that the apostrophe use required is one of contraction but that there is either an omission (for example, missing from 'Its widely known that ...') or an error ('Its' widely known that ...'). Any instances of apostrophe use highlighted in pink signal that apostrophes of possession are needed but have either been omitted (for example, 'Fergusons view is ...') or there is an error ('Fergusons' view is ...'). Use of blue to highlight an item indicates that an apostrophe has been used where it is not needed, most commonly attached to plural nouns (for example, 'the views' of young people'). It is a useful technique which helps pupils notice apostrophe use and signals the various forms of error, as well as confirming accurate use which many pupils demonstrate some of the time perhaps through guesswork resulting from incomplete understanding.

Barney explains the highlighting technique and the significance of the colours. He provides examples of the different types of error drawn from pupils' work. This is always anonymised. Around each example he explains which function of apostrophe is required, to signal possession or contraction, and he sometimes elicits opinions from the pupils. Usually their explanations seem secure but for some pupils it seems they hazard a guess, with a fifty–fifty chance of accuracy. The explanations Barney provides are accurate and expressed clearly, though this doesn't prevent the feeling that some pupils don't understand, and continue not to understand, despite the quality and patience of Barney's comments.

Barney continues, introducing an exercise in which pupils are presented with ten sentences. All require the addition of apostrophes, though there is no indication of where these should fall or what their function might be. Barney expects pupils to use their judgement to decide where the apostrophes should go. He guides them in the first example and every pupil annotates the sentence, inserting the apostrophe in the correct place. Across the next five minutes pupils work individually, placing commas in each of the remaining nine sentences. To an observer, it is the picture of industry: all pupils are quiet and focused on their worksheets, visibly on task. It is only when pupils finish and Barney guides them in checking their answers that he finds there remains confusion about apostrophe use, or at least around their use in the examples on the worksheet. For each item considered, at least a third of the pupils signal an incorrect choice when asked to signal through a show of hands agreement with various possibilities.

Because his lesson has other objectives as the priority, Barney says to his class that he'll take in the worksheets and that 'apostrophes will be something we will return to soon'. He then begins the lesson proper, introducing a topic to stimulate writing for argument and explanation.

Review of Barney's lesson, including review of research on apostrophe use

This section presents options for Barney that are research-based, first describing research that directly considered approaches to teaching apostrophes. It then presents two options which not only take account of this specialised study, but also reflect the different models of grammar teaching described above. One option tends to the discrete and explicit method of grammar teaching, while the other embeds teaching about apostrophe use within the writing process.

One study (Bryant et al., 2000: 273) recognised a phenomenon consistent with Barney's findings and familiar to many teachers, that 'English speaking children find it difficult to learn about the use of the apostrophe to denote possession'. It called coming to terms with the apostrophe 'a formidable developmental hurdle'. The research found that 'many of the

children who did badly in the spelling task used the apostrophe pro-
fusely: the trouble in their case was that they used it with inappropriate
words very nearly as often as with appropriate ones'. This too is in tune
with what Barney's marking revealed: most pupils use it correctly sometimes but not consistently. The study also had implications for pedagogy,
finding that many of the children continued to find apostrophe use difficult 'even after more than a year's instruction'. In that light, pupils' apparent lack of progress in Barney's lesson is not surprising.

Why did problems for pupils in the study continue? The authors
argue that a key factor was pupils' limited awareness of the apostrophe
as a unit of meaning (in their tests, to denote possession), possibly
because they had not spoken about language in terms of units of meaning before. Instead, their framework for thinking about language was
dominated by attention to sound-letter (phono-graphemic) correspond-
ences, an emphasis sympathetic with systematic phonics. An awareness of language as units of meaning, on the other hand, constitutes
morphology. Around apostrophes, these pupils failed to 'recognise the
morphemic distinction involved'. The authors posit 'a specific and long
lasting connection between children's morpho-syntactic awareness and
their eventual success with apostrophes'. They based this conclusion
on the results of a test in which children's use of 'morpho-syntactic'
awareness was called upon, though surprisingly it did not require use of
genitive words (possessive forms using the apostrophe, such as 'Sarah's
book'). Nevertheless, there was a correlation between pupils' performance in this test and pupils' later accurate use of the apostrophe.
Bryant et al. (2000: 273) conclude that this suggests:

> an independent form of linguistic awareness, which is awareness of
> morphemes. The connection is also exciting because the use of the
> apostrophe in English to denote possession is pure morphology.
> The apostrophe only signifies a morpheme: it represents no sound.

The implications for teaching are that pupils must be able to recognise
words which are genitive and those which are not if they are to use
apostrophes correctly. They are likely to benefit from teaching that
explicitly attends to the apostrophe as a unit of meaning, and more
broadly of the 'conventional spelling for morphemes'. In teaching apostrophe use this could entail describing the morphemic principles relevant
to the pronouns 'his', 'hers', 'its', 'theirs' and 'ours', and their relationship
with genitive forms such as 'the teacher's knowledge', 'the school's grammar policy' and 'the pupils' progress'.

Barney's first option – discrete teaching of apostrophe use

The very principle of a free-standing starter activity like the one in Barney's lesson confirms the widespread influence of the discrete model of grammar teaching. The introduction of starter activities on a national scale coincided with the introduction of the Secondary Framework for Literacy in the late 1990s. As the National Literacy Strategy was transformed from its primary-phase template for deployment at secondary level, lessons with four phases ('the four-part lesson') became the dominant mode of lesson design. The parts were starter, then introduction, development and plenary. Though the template did not preclude connections between the starter and later phases, starters were often treated as self-contained ten-minute sections set aside for quick bursts of grammar and spelling work. The guidance for associated Literacy Progress Units of the era confirms this tendency. Though these resources were devised first as catch-up interventions for pupils performing below expected levels for their age group, often taught in small groups withdrawn from whole-class lessons, the supporting notes suggested the material could be adapted to form starters for full classes. Most of the units concentrated on aspects of grammar and spelling, addressed in brief teaching sessions. Where these were used with small groups, the scripted schedules usually lasted 20 minutes. Aside from the official resources, disseminated through heavily structured centralised training, independent publishers joined in to provide a plethora of starter activity packs for every dimension of grammar teaching articulated in the prescriptive (though not statutory) secondary framework objectives. These often took the form of photocopiable tasks across a single side of A4 paper. Teaching about language usually conformed to the formula 'grammar and spelling = starter + worksheet', sometimes incorporating mini-whiteboards to support rapid feedback.

Barney's starter activity derives from the same tradition. The validity of the approach he has taken with this format is supported by the research specific to apostrophe use, which urges deliberate and explicit attention to apostrophes in teaching, and by one of the 'high-quality' studies cited in the 2004 systematic review insofar as it encourages 'using strategies for labelling and identifying grammatical features' followed by practice using these, in response to which the teacher should provide feedback. Barney already has most of these components in his teaching. The assessment he made of pupils' use of apostrophes has the potential to be a very powerful feedback mechanism, though he would have improved that impact by deferring its use. Teaching apostrophes explicitly with some reference to the categories he used in connection with the highlighter colours could help pupils recognise the different functions, especially if he were to refine the categories and introduce them in a more systematic manner, devoting more time to each area.

One opportunity lies in exploring the correspondence of possessive (and genitive) uses of the apostrophe with the possessive pronouns. It may be of help to isolate this function of the apostrophe in this context, and address it in a lesson separate from one considering the contracting function of the apostrophe. One risk of covering apostrophe use in one go, detailing both functions, is to always present them together and possibly to consolidate the confusion for pupils. In that approach, pupils encounter both uses and explanations almost simultaneously, and the two are bound together. If separated, one function can be dealt with in relation to genitive principles, and so the common function of meaning becomes the focus for learning rather than the apostrophe per se. Such a lesson might consider possessive pronouns, use of the possessive apostrophe in singular and plural forms, and constructions of possession using the preposition 'of', such as 'the brother of John'. This affords opportunity to mitigate muddle over apostrophe use in the possessive 'its' and the contraction of 'it is' as 'it's'. Attention is given to 'its' as a possessive pronoun, similar to 'his', 'her' and 'our' (but not 'their') in having three letters but no apostrophe. The common patterning may offer the most powerful trigger for pupils to note the shared function. Pupils could also be introduced to a test of substitution. If they are presented with sentences like 'The horse made its way along the road' and 'It's a very sunny day', they can see if substitution of the item with another possessive pronoun would maintain sense and syntax. If it does, then 'its' with no apostrophe is likely to be the correct use.

Another lesson on the apostrophe of contraction can also exploit grouping to emphasise the function as the focus for learning. If the learning objective is not to understand apostrophes but instead to know common forms of contraction, the apostrophe per se is once again the secondary concern. The teacher may decide to address the most common contractions, for example where the apostrophe signals an omitted 'i' (in 'it's' and 'there's') or a missing 'o' ('didn't'). The former can be introduced through contractions that are indicative of location, possibly with the help of deixis: 'Where's my lottery ticket?', 'There's your tenner', 'Here's my fiver', 'It's a lucky day'. The second group could feature in a sequence of dialogue (perhaps using *Rosencrantz and Guildenstern Are Dead*'s verbal tennis as a model?): Don't give her that; Won't she like it?; I haven't a clue; Why can't you tell me?; I couldn't possibly … and so on.

Barney's second option – embedded teaching of apostrophe use

Barney could look to the work of the *Grammar for Writing?* project as the basis for this approach. The descriptions of the research procedure offer detailed explanation of what embedded or 'contextualised grammar' means in practice in terms of resource design and classroom activity. The team devised schemes that emphasised points of grammar relevant to the genre for study and its distinctive features. By 'contextualised grammar', the team meant introducing grammatical constructions and terminology where it was directly relevant to pupils' immediate writing process. By implication this makes grammar teaching intermittent, spread across the scheme. Lessons would not, by contrast, deal with all the relevant grammar issues in one go at the start of the scheme, detached from everything else. Grammar points would be woven in, with a focus 'on effects and constructing meanings, not on the feature or terminology itself'. The approach entails introducing terminology through examples (and patterns evident across several instances); reflecting on how grammar choices improve the impact of writing; imitating model patterns demonstrated in real texts; and encouraging play and experimentation with language as key to helping pupils develop judgement as 'designers' of writing. Clearly the approach aims to avoid a tick-box approach whereby pupils simply spot features in examples and in their own work, instead developing an understanding that whatever language they use represents a choice of many options.

The schemes used in the project covered three written genres (narrative fiction, argument and poetry) covered in the English curriculum. The scheme on argument included an initial lesson on counter-argument, using a game 'focused on anticipating and dismissing any objections to an idea before they could scupper an argument'. In particular, pupils had to use a 'yes, but' construction, which led into consideration of a wider range of connectives useful for engaging in argument. In the next task, pupils were given an example of writing to argue in the form of an article about keeping a dangerous pet. In a card-sort activity they experimented with placing connectives at the start or in the middle of sentences, 'exploring the different patterns of emphasis created by placing main clauses at the start or the end of a sentence'. Crucially, pupils were asked to consider the communicative impact of their choices: which allowed most successful dismissal of negative arguments and which placed emphasis on positive points most effectively? The same task afforded attention to subordinating and coordinating connectives, to their role in emphasising one clause over another, and to the use of commas relative to subordinate clauses used to start sentences. The result was a collection of 'entertaining pieces which argued that they should be allowed to keep a dangerous animal as a pet, focusing on pre-empting any arguments that might be used against them'. A second lesson in the scheme concentrated on how modal verbs affect the tone of a sentence, 'the ways in which they express degrees of possibility, how they can muse or suggest, wheedle or bribe, or sound strong, definite and inspirational'.

If Barney is to guide pupils on apostrophe use in the spirit of con-textualised grammar, he will only do so where it is relevant to the writing in which he guides pupils. As with the first option, this is likely to favour attending to the distinct functions of apostrophe use, but in this case the function emphasised will depend on the text genre for study. If he engages pupils in the common task of writing copy for a holiday brochure or tourist guide, consideration of the possessive apostrophe is likely to complement the use of personal pronouns. This real example from the Visit Norfolk website includes both:

> The city's historic street layout is wonderfully haphazard, but there's no need to get lost, just look for the obvious landmarks – the spire of the majestic Norman Cathedral, the domineering castle on its tall mound and City Hall's clock tower.

You may have noticed the apostrophe of contraction too. Barney could deal with that here but would probably lend his teaching further impact if he addressed contraction in a form that uses it more frequently. Prohibitive signs or rules would be relevant. There could even be an engaging tension in a holiday unit that permits both of these suggestions: first, idealising a resort in hyperbolic brochure copy, then revealing the true face of the resort in the restrictive house rules of a very unwelcoming hotel with a fondness for the 'don't' construction.

Conclusion

While the debate around approaches to grammar teaching tends to present poles of opinion and suggest that teaching grammar is a matter of dogma, in practice most teachers adopt a mixture of approaches. This chapter has demonstrated two choices open to Barney, but he could very easily draw from each across a term. It may help him to be aware of the processes his pupils knew at primary school and build on these if at all possible. In his own assessment of pupils' grammar, he will need to be alert to the difference between pupils knowing points of grammar and their capacity to demonstrate their accurate use in practice.

References

Andrews, Richard, Torgerson, Carole, Beverton, Sue, Locke Terry, Low, Graham, Robinson, Alison and Zhu, Die (2004) *The Effect of Grammar Teaching (Syntax) in English on 5 to 16 Year Olds' Accuracy and Quality in Written Composition*, Research Evidence in Education Library. London: EPPI-Centre, Social Science Research Unit, Institute of Education.

Bryant, Peter, Nunes, Terezinha and Bindman, Miriam (2000) 'The relations between children's linguistic awareness and spelling: the case of the apostrophe', *Reading and Writing: An Interdisciplinary Journal*, 12: 253–76.

DfE (2013) *English Programmes of Study: Key Stage 3 (National Curriculum in England)*. Reference: DFE-00184-2013.

DfEE (1999) *The National Curriculum: Key Stages 3 and 4*. London: QCA.

Gove, Michael (2010) Speech to the Conservative Party Conference, Birmingham, 5 October.; online at: http://centrallobby.politicshome.com/latestnews/article-detail/newsarticle/speech-in-full-michael-gove/. (accessed 1 October 2014)

Independent, The (2012) 'Headteachers vote to expel Michael Gove's new reading tests'; online at: http://www.independent.co.uk/news/education/education-news/headteachers-vote-to-expel-michael-goves-new-reading-tests-for-primary-school-pupils-7718685.html. (accessed 1 October 2014)

Jones, Susan, Myhill, Debra and Bailey, Trevor (2013) 'Grammar for writing? An investigation of the effects of contextualised grammar teaching on students' writing', *Reading and Writing*, 26 (8): 1241–63.

Mirror, The (2013) 'Michael Gove given lesson in grammar by schoolgirl who spotted errors in exam paper'; online at: http://www.mirror.co.uk/news/uk-news/michael-gove-given-lesson-grammar-189566. (accessed 1 December 2013)

National Literacy Trust (2014) *Children's Enjoyment of Reading*; online at: http://www.literacytrust.org.uk/news/6079_children_s_enjoyment_of_reading_has_increased_for_the_first_time_in_eight_years. (accessed 1 October 2014)

Ofqual (2013) *GCSE Reform*; online at: ofqual.gov.uk/qualifications-and-assessments/qualification-reform/gcse-reform/. (accessed 1 October 2014)

Telegraph, The (2012) 'Young people more likely to judge spelling and grammar online'; online at: http://www.telegraph.co.uk/technology/social-media/9730293/Young-more-likely-to-judge-spelling-and-grammar-online.html. (accessed 1 October 2014)

CHAPTER 7

MEDIA AND MULTILITERACIES IN ENGLISH

Objectives of this chapter:

- To explain the relationship between the new curriculum and media education
- To introduce approaches to media texts that match curricular requirements
- To identify scope for media teaching in English that recognises the distinctiveness of media texts
- To suggest resources to support your teaching of media texts

Introduction: the 2014 curriculum and media education

The National Curriculum has since its inception in 1989 included a programme of study headed 'Reading'. Across the 1990s and first decade of this century, the details for this domain developed from a focus on print media to recognise more fully the relevance of audio-visual texts and, in effect, came to encompass a statutory though slight entitlement for all pupils to media education. The current programmes of study (DfE, 2013, 2014) for each key stage have brought further changes. What place does media education have in the current details?

In contrast with the curriculum introduced under Labour (DfEE, 1999) and its subsequent iterations (for example, through the *Framework for Secondary English* (DCFS, 2008)), the present curriculum omits any overt mention of moving-image texts. The overall aims of the curriculum make clear that the focus is now on print-based texts, emphasising literature and, in non-fiction, 'reading for information'. The curriculum thus states these broad aims, for pupils:

- to read easily, fluently and with good understanding;
- to develop the habit of reading widely and often, for both pleasure and information; and
- to acquire a wide vocabulary, an understanding of grammar and knowledge of linguistic conventions for reading, writing and spoken language.

The literary emphasis of the new details is further apparent in these broad requirements which insist that pupils should be taught to:

> develop an appreciation and love of reading, and read increasingly challenging material independently through: reading a wide range of fiction and non-fiction, including in particular whole books, short stories, poems and plays with a wide coverage of genres, historical periods, forms and authors. (DfE, 2013: 4)

The requirements specify the forms of 'prose, poetry and drama' and a range that includes 'Shakespeare (two plays)' and 'seminal world literature'. Pupils will chose and read 'books independently for challenge, interest and enjoyment'.

There are no signals here to suggest that any texts other than those in print are accorded value by the new arrangements. The opening statement asserts that 'all the skills of language are essential to participating fully as a member of society; pupils, therefore, who do not learn to speak, read and write fluently and confidently are effectively disenfranchised.' In the context of global developments in information technology, the modern media environment and the concept of multiliteracies, there is a possibility that English pupils may enjoy only partial enfranchisement as an outcome of their curriculum-based learning. If it is effective they will be equipped to use the English language 'fluently so that they can communicate their ideas and emotions to others'. They will also be receptive to how 'others can communicate with them' through what they hear and what they read. However, there is a significant dimension of their everyday world that does not appear to be addressed in the English curriculum, or for that matter in any part of the revised curriculum structure.

This is an irony given some of the phrases found later in the document, which describe 'increasingly challenging texts' and the ability to 'read critically'. A great deal of valued recent research and commentary has recognised the complexity and challenge of interpreting and producing texts that work across various modes, often including but not limited to print. At the same time, multimodal texts have been closely associated with 'critical literacy', especially relative to the potential democratising impact of the Internet and mobile technology which complicate simple dichotomies of author/reader and speaking/writing. The new curricular details for English point in the other direction, highlighting the authority of the author and reasserting a canon worthy (by its own terms) of our consideration.

Gwen's lesson design

Gwen's lesson with a Year 9 class is about advertisements. In it she gives pupils the opportunity to look at advertisements in two media, print and the moving image. The recent revisions to the National Curriculum emphasise printed texts in the Reading programme of study, so Gwen parallels that balance in her own lesson. Nevertheless, her work with the moving image remains important in preparing pupils with the skills to read advertisements they will encounter in many different forms beyond the classroom, whether in magazines, through viral campaigns or on television. The outline Gwen presents for her lesson is concisely expressed, as follows:

Learning objectives

1. To know the main features of advertisements.
2. To analyse features of advertisements.
3. To understand the effect of language and images and their link with the text's purpose and target audience.

Figure 7.1 shows Gwen's lesson plan as she expressed it on paper.

Phase	Duration (minutes)	Activity
1	5	Introduction to the learning objectives.
2	5	Teacher eliciting pupils' ideas about what adverts do and checking their understanding of target audience.
3	5	Viewing moving-image advertisements – pupils must identify possible target audience and explain how the clip appeals to them in order to sell the product. Take responses from pupils after each clip.
4	10	Discuss persuasive techniques in the examples and if possible from wider knowledge. Pupils copy list of techniques from PowerPoint presentation.
5	25	Present pupils with advertisements for analysis, suggesting target audience and answering questions about techniques used in each. Teacher will first demonstrate how to do the activity with an example shown to the class, and model the response using the note-making grid (5 mins). Pupils have four minutes looking at each advert and completing the column on their grid, then adverts will be passed on in rotation.
6	10	Plenary – pupils share comment about each advert (around a minute devoted to each), then final question asking pupils to describe the differing effects of two of the adverts, also explaining how language and images contribute to those effects.

Figure 7.1 Gwen's lesson design for teaching about advertisements

Gwen's lesson as it was taught

The lesson starts with a now conventional phase of introducing the objectives verbatim, just as they are presented above, through a presentation on a PowerPoint slide. Gwen reads each one aloud to the pupils before asking them to copy all three. She then poses the opening question orally: *What do advertisements do?* Her pupils offer some ideas through 'hands-up' contributions: 'they try to sell us things', 'they can make us laugh', 'some can be annoying'. Gwen advances her PowerPoint presentation to a slide that includes three suggestions that show she anticipated some of the pupils' ideas:

> *What do advertisements do?*
> They tell us about the product.
> They explain what a product is for.
> They aim to persuade us to buy the product.

One difference from some of the pupil contributions is that these purposes tend to link with the promoter's intentions, while two of the pupils' remarks above recognise what advertisements can do in terms of effect on their audience. This emphasis is confirmed when Gwen asks a rhetorical question about what else advertisers need to consider, for which she provides the answer 'target audience'. Gwen asks her class *What do I mean by target audience?* and the first pupil invited to respond offers 'the people the advert is aimed at'. Gwen accepts this as the correct answer and very clearly expresses her endorsement: 'yes, good answer, spot on'.

Gwen continues, marking a transition: 'We are going to look at three television advertisements. For each one I want you to tell me who you think the target audience might be. I'd also like you to think about how the adverts appeal to you, and how much they are likely to persuade you to buy the products.' She shows them the advertisements in turn, pausing after each one to elicit suggestions about the target audience and then to encourage pupils' more general observations about their persuasive impact.

The first advertisement is a fairly generic 30-second example for a Ford car (incubate-innovation.org, 2013). It closes with the spoken rhetorical question 'Twenty-four hours with a new Ford Fiesta, with revolutionary EcoBoost engine technology – what would you do?' This follows sequences depicting 'the twenty-four hour Fiesta project', in which the artist Rafaël Rozendaal effectively makes the car into an installation, similar to those on show at his own website. This involves coating the vehicle in white paint, surrounding it with shattered glass, and projecting onto it various colours, mostly primary. The car is thus illuminated in colour, highlighting it against darkened surroundings.

The second advertisement is for Galaxy chocolate. The minute-long commercial depicts a CGI-rendered Audrey Hepburn taking a bus ride along a 1950s Amalfi coastline (see independent.co.uk, 2013, for video and related article). The bus is stopped and delayed as a rustic Italian grocer's stall has collapsed and blocked its way, fruit and vegetables strewing the road. Audrey takes a lift with a passing motorist in his silver Mercedes convertible, Henry Mancini's *Moon River* plays in the background, and sunlight glints off the car as it speeds into the distance. As she sits in the back, she enjoys a piece of chocolate. The advert concludes with the tagline, 'Why have cotton when you can have silk?'

The final advert is one of a series produced for Go Compare, a price comparison website, available to view on their website (http://gocompare.com, 2014). This example shows the opera tenor character (Gio Compario, appearing throughout the series) speaking with a woman at a bus stop. He bemoans the lack of attention he receives, 'All I'm trying to do is to help people save up to £290 on their car insurance' and asks 'And what do I get?', which is followed by flashbacks of someone apparently shooting at him with a bazooka, him being hit in the stomach with a football and finally him being caught in a mantrap which restrains him in a net and lifts him from the ground. He concludes 'Why people don't listen to me I will never know', and the woman responds sarcastically, 'Yeah, it's a mystery'. The advertisement closes with two captions, the first reinforcing the £290 saving and the second providing the slogan 'Go Compare – saving the nation'.

The pupils are enthusiastic about the advertisements, and it is possible to hear several exclamations of 'Oh I love this!' and 'This is well funny'. Gwen gently directs the pupils to concentrate on the films and as soon as the clips finish she tries to get answers about the relevant target audiences. Often the answers she receives are quite brief or underdeveloped: 'that one is for people who like chocolate', 'that one would be for older people I think, maybe like my dad or someone like that', and 'that one is for people who want insurance'. The first and last of these conflate the target audience with the product, and though to a degree correct, show that the pupils are not able to make a precise suggestion about the nature of each target audience. The second example demonstrates a slightly more sophisticated understanding, as it indicates both a concept of age group and gender.

As Gwen takes responses from pupils about aspects of the advertisements that might persuade them to buy the product, she notes down ideas on the board. These include 'it's funny', 'it makes me think it is a good car' and 'it makes you think eating the chocolate is fun'. At the same time, some pupils take a pragmatic approach based on their own experience by this age: 'I wouldn't buy the car anyway 'cause I can't drive yet', or 'I wouldn't spend my money on insurance'.

Next, Gwen shares with pupils a slide that lists various features of advertisements under the heading 'persuasive devices'. The list includes slogans, puns, alliteration, rhetorical questions, imperatives and personal pronouns, together with colour, images and 'sounds/music'. Gwen asks pupils to copy the list into their books then introduces the next and most lengthy activity of the lesson. In this phase pupils look at print-based advertisements which are in a single-page format drawn from magazines and newspapers. Gwen does not make the shift from audio-visual examples to the print medium explicit to pupils. There is potential for pupils to be confused by the relevance to these new examples of 'sounds/music' as a persuasive device.

Because the classroom is organised with pupils sitting around five different tables, Gwen is able to use a rotation activity where each group works with a different advert, passing them round to the next table at timed intervals. Gwen shows the whole class what to do in the activity by presenting an advertisement for all to see via the projector, and populating a format designed to capture data about each advertisement. In a column for each of the five advertisements, Gwen asks pupils to enter details for each of these categories:

Product advertised
Describe the image
What words are included and what is their effect?
Who is the target audience?
How successful do you think the advert is?

The pupils then have five minutes to look at each advertisement, consider it as a group and fill in the boxes of the table with the relevant information. In their first go, pupils take longer than five minutes and need frequent prompting from Gwen to move on from one box to the next. In the second rotation, the class generally do better though a couple of groups take longer with their examples than others. By the third rotation the groups are more or less synchronised. The activity appears to work well by this point, and though the full activity takes longer than Gwen planned, every pupil has a chance to see each advert and talk about it. Some pupils have empty boxes for one or two of the advertisements, showing that in some cases their groups didn't get to the last two questions. If they did, they were either unsure about how to answer and articulate their thoughts in writing, or perhaps didn't understand what was required. In terms of organisation and managing pupils' focus so it was directed to the task, Gwen did very well and can count the practical arrangement of the activity a success.

Finally, Gwen asks one person from each table to talk about one of the adverts, and as the class listen to each one the advert Gwen designates for comment alters so that feedback is received on each one. She then asks the groups to choose two adverts they felt had different effects and to explain why. She has time to hear from two groups which both seem able to express the different effects quite well in informal terms.

Written feedback from Gwen's mentor

I really liked this lesson and the range of material you used. The pupils often recognised the advertisements or at least the products and that stimulated their conversation about advertising. You managed the

(Continued)

(Continued)

rotation activity well so that everyone kept to time and conversations remained focused on the task.

One effect of using several advertisements like this is that it takes pupils some time to read and 'tune-in' to each one as they are circulated. Your objectives are all linked to the single idea of persuasion, so to keep it in pupils' minds it would be useful to mention 'persuasion' frequently and at every stage. You could include a starting question about persuasion in your list, perhaps a direct question such as 'Do you find the advertisement at all persuasive?' Even before adverts persuade you to do something they have to gain attention, so a first question might even be 'How well does this advert persuade you to give it your attention?' If you maintain the rotation activity, that means they will reflect on persuasion at least five times. In later plenary work, they will be prepared to answer an evaluative question such as 'Which did you find most persuasive?'.

All of these questions invite pupils' personal response, which is an essential step towards analysis. In the first part of the lesson you noted on your plan that you hoped pupils might draw on their wider knowledge of adverts and you could direct that more, e.g. by asking them to recall an advertisement they enjoyed. It would be a good first activity to let them recount the advert to another pupil, and to explain why they enjoyed it and perhaps why they remembered it too. By succeeding in entertaining, any example they talk about has already succeeded in persuading them to give it their attention. They can develop comment to describe the product or service it describes. It is possible, even from an early stage in the lesson, that if they are talking about an advert that engages them they will also be able to remark on how it appeals to them and its likely target audience.

One thing to consider for future development is how the purpose of persuasion merits some unpacking itself. You made some connections with prior work on newspaper articles, where readers were also persuaded, though more in terms of outlook or beliefs. If you think about how everything you do frames and influences how pupils talk and write about persuasion, you can do things from the outset that will help them respond in precise and subtle ways. Though it is fair to say that most advertisements aim to persuade us to buy or use a given service or product, they can do this with varied and often sophisticated techniques.

Pupils are likely to see with ease the persuasive intent of an advertisement that overtly declares a special offer or which signals a discount of cost for a product. They are less likely to recognise as persuasive those advertisements that simply place the brand in front of us, to keep it in mind and keep it current, raising its profile and establishing it as necessary or normal. These are the advertisements that treat brands almost as institutions – for example Nike ads, which may not promote a single product but promote the entire company. These ads also build brand image and suggest associated values, positioning products and services as lifestyle choices. If you can find and include in your lesson advertisements that fulfil varying functions like these, and sum up the distinct functions in carefully worded explanations, you can help pupils be more alert to nuanced persuasive texts that work as part of wider campaigns as well as on their own. In some units you teach on advertising, campaigns themselves can be a useful means of lending unity to the work. Frequently they include advertisements that work across several media, and it is quite possible that you will also find published material describing their rationale, target audience and sometimes evaluations of their impact.

Resources available to Gwen for her teaching

The tutor's comments suggest plenty for Gwen to consider for her continuing work around adverting but do not specify materials on which she might draw. Gwen would probably find the Thinkbox website (Thinkbox, 2014) very useful. As the site explains, 'Thinkbox is the marketing body for commercial TV in the UK, in all its forms – broadcast, on-demand and interactive.' The site comprises some examples of advertisements, including collected examples drawn from campaigns. In addition, it includes useful information about the aims and impact of television advertising, as well as data about audience viewing habits. A glossary of advertising industry terminology is of potential practical use during teaching, as are various data charts indicating patterns of viewing and audience response. Perhaps most useful of all is its section devoted to advertising case studies, which show how companies have successfully marketed their products or services by identifying 'the challenge' of reaching an audience, describing the actions taken in response (as 'the TV solution') and concluding with comment on 'the impact'. While the advertisements at the heart of each case study are readily accessible resources in themselves, the supporting commentaries can inform Gwen's knowledge of their use in context. She can call on this overtly if she chooses, sharing some of the details with pupils, or she may simply wish to be aware of these details so that she can draw on them spontaneously as necessary when she works with her classes. Elsewhere, 'galleries' of advertisements are collected around shared themes, for example for Christmas products, advertisements related to football and promotional material for major brands. Another section considers 'TV effectiveness': though it does not analyse language features in the manner of Gwen's lesson, it introduces aspects relevant to their persuasive function which encompass the institutional arrangements of their creation and how effectiveness is proven, and with what evidence, within the industry.

Using this material, Gwen can modify her teaching so that it becomes more than an exercise that only occurs within the English classroom. It improves so that it is properly informed by current industry practice, and the knowledge pupils acquire can be relevant to informed careers advice and to wider citizenship matters. Gwen may even opt to make clear to pupils who funds and produces the Thinkbox site, the pages of which explain:

> Its shareholders are Channel 4, ITV, Sky Media, Turner Media Innovations and UKTV, who together represent over 90% of commercial TV advertising revenue through their owned and partner TV channels. RTL Group and Virgin Media are Associate Members and Discovery Channel UK & STV also give direct financial support. Thinkbox works with the marketing community with a single ambition: to help advertisers get the best out of today's TV.

The material on the site offers the possibility of advertising work extending beyond reading and analysing texts in a quite conventional, traditional vein. It begins to encompass critical literacy (see Morgan, 1997), addressing the motives and circumstances of production as well as texts themselves.

A rationale for Gwen's work: media education and citizenship

Ofsted (2013) states that a large number of pupils do not see the relevance of English to their lives outside school, or the relevance of what they do in lessons to later employment. Some commentators frame the argument for media education around its potential in these terms, claiming that preparation for life beyond school is inherent in a wider conception of literacy, or rather multiliteracies. This approach views communication as multimodal, constituted of linguistic, visual, audio, spatial and gestural skills. It reflects the full range of skills required of leisure and professional life in the contemporary world: young people must be multiliterate to thrive.

'Multiliteracies' was the term coined by a group of scholars who labelled themselves the New London Group (Cazden et al., 1996), developed in the context of globalisation and the new forms of communication that arise from developing technologies. To be multiliterate is to have the capacity to understand many types of text, which are likely to work across more than one mode of communication. Texts are therefore often 'multimodal', deploying linguistic, visual, audio, spatial and gestural elements. The multiliteracy framework proposed by the New London Group offers:

> a metalanguage that describes meaning in various realms. These include the textual and the visual, as well as the multimodal relations between the different meaning-making processes that are now so critical in media texts and the texts of electronic media. (Cazden et al., 1996)

Modern technology can provide greater and more immediate access to other cultures than ever before. A world which is globalised as a result fosters and requires a greater awareness of diversity. As governments and institutions modify their own operations to make use of online and mobile resources, educational institutions have modified their own ways of working. The skill set needed by pupils has changed in the last couple of decades and continues to change.

Many territories design curricula to embody with increasing depth the plurality of multiliteracies. The rationale statement for the Australia senior secondary curriculum for English encompasses 'viewing', 'listening' and 'modes' (http://australiancurriculum.edu.au, 2014), New Zealand's details emphasise 'visual texts' (http://nzcurriculum.tki.org.nz) and an example from Canada for Ontario describes the centrality of a variety of media texts (Ontario Ministry of Education, 2007: 4–5) and cites UNESCO's own broad conception of literacy:

> Literacy is about more than reading or writing – it is about how we communicate in society. It is about social practices and relationships, about knowledge, language and culture. (UNESCO, Statement for the United Nations Literacy Decade, 2003–2012)

Concurrently, the formal English curriculum for England and Wales moves further away from developing conceptions of literacy intended to keep pace with the demands of language use in a changing world. Despite Ofsted's evidence about the uncertainty young people have about the usefulness of English as a discipline, it reasserts a print-based view of literacy emphasising a narrow canon of literary texts and finding scant room for the moving image. If we explore the new curriculum's professed aim of preventing 'disenfranchisement' and frame that positively as a matter of enfranchisement, the scope of English teaching has to look beyond print alone.

Institutions of government and education can influence enfranchisement, but so do the media. According to CivicWeb (2007), citizens and hence pupils 'need skills and knowledge about how media works, how he or she can participate, and also the willingness and courage to engage in civic culture'. For as long as the official curriculum omits recognition of modern media and corresponding forms of communication, it runs the risk of failing to equip young people with the skills and confidence to participate in the media-rich 'civic culture' (see Dahlgren, 2007a, 2007b; Dahlgren and Olsson, 2007). While the online world has meant already politically-minded individuals have become more active, there has been little effect on those prone to disengagement. This suggests that curriculum design has to acknowledge the need to address media-based enfranchisement explicitly if it is to have any impact on the status quo. The report for the UK project Children Go Online (Livingstone and Bober, 2005) recommended that institutions seeking the participation of young people develop genuinely interactive environments to secure engagement, the perspective of young people vividly articulated in the remark that many civic sites are just 'chunks and chunks of writing, no narrative, personal stories, no real people, no games'. Buckingham (2000, 2003) found that media education that included online journalism and discussion supported youth engagement in local culture. The later CHICAM project (Children in Communication about Migration) suggested the importance of access to technology in effective and structured media literacy programmes (de Block and Sefton-Green, 2004).

Assuming that Gwen continues to teach advertising within her first teaching post, what can she do with it that meets curricular requirements but which might also meet broader educational aims? What can she do to encompass media-oriented and civic literacy in her approach?

Transforming Gwen's lesson

The multiliteracies paradigm makes clear that empowerment through literacy today extends beyond the ability to read and use the written word, though even the traditional print texts of the curriculum can provide an opportunity to examine the way texts work across various modes. A sonnet, for instance, is far more than simply a linguistic text. It operates spatially too, in its presentation as a square block of print on the page. A print advertisement will often combine language and image, while a novel may exploit sequential opportunities. These examples suggest that a multiliteracy framework could fulfil the requirements of the current curriculum and more, permitting attention to traditional forms and canonised texts as well as nascent media and ephemeral communication.

Gwen can apply this ethos to advertising in various ways, maintaining some use of the moving image while recognising the apparent emphasis of curricular requirements on verbal and usually written detail. Like some of the websites mentioned above, 'chunks and chunks' of writing will dominate, words being the mode receiving most attention. The curriculum makes no overt reference to aural and visual modes and so these must be treated as peripheral relative to the official framework. Still, the curriculum requires 'reading with good understanding' and that pupils read 'challenging material independently'. Using advertisements as moving-image texts can support both and inform a deeper understanding of print texts. It would be acceptable, for instance, to consider texts drawn from a single advertising campaign, providing the case study comprised texts with sufficient verbal content. As well as advertisements intended for magazines or newspapers, this could include transcripts of radio advertisements and moving image advertisements that feature substantial amounts of dialogue or equally prominent commentary as voiceover. In such a context, even those texts with slighter use of verbal modes are useful.

Gwen could guide pupils in an exploration of how the same or similar messages are conveyed across the *range* of texts. In Gwen's original lesson the advertisements had no common thread. This approach provides coherence but also some variety, with gentle distinctions that can help pupils understand how texts communicate comparable content. It can help pupils a great deal to have a contrast through juxtaposition: what information does the print advertisement include that the moving-image advertisement does not? How does the print advertisement present in words information that may be communicated through images in the television ad? The comparison of at least two differing examples also provides a clear structure for analysis, which also mirrors a format common to literary analysis where pupils consider two poems together. The website of the History of Advertising Trust (HAT) is an excellent place for Gwen to seek material about advertising campaigns in addition to the resources of Thinkbox described earlier. Its collections comprise advertising in most media formats. HAT's specialism in advertising through time also means that it includes ample material pre-dating the moving image, making it possible to compare advertisements for the same product that may be decades apart. That too gives an opportunity to contrast an older verbal text with a more recent multimodal example, but also to exploit resources in very different ways for the wider English curriculum. Advertisements contemporary to World War One, for instance, can be means to understand the social context and – in terms of critical literacy – to examine propaganda, perhaps before looking at more subtle modern examples.

The CivicWeb project highlighted the engagement of young people when they have scope to produce texts. The interplay of moving-image texts and print examples provides an opportunity to work around the transformation of texts, involving pupils in transposing a message from one form to another. If the curriculum relegates moving images to the status of stimuli, at least Gwen can engage her pupils in thoughtful and perceptive reading by asking them to think about how the message of a television advertisement would need to change if it were to be conveyed in print. Pupils can demonstrate their understanding as producers, composing the print version. In isolation this could lack rigour, as it could easily omit attention to the target audience. If initial study of the moving image identifies and explores how it appeals to its intended viewers, the quality of initial work here can be improved.

One quite simple method would be to provide pupils with a magazine or newspaper, for which they identify and describe the intended audience. Their suggestions can be informed by the content, including advertisements already found there. Gwen could also provide them with more detailed information about the readership, perhaps based on demographic data (the Thinkbox website is very thorough in this respect). If the production task is designed so that the target audience here is markedly different from the audience of the television advertisement, pupils have to transform the message for a new mode and manipulate language to have a different appeal. She could allocate different magazines to different pupils or groups, so that the class can explore the distinctiveness of the transformations. This underlines the strong link between audience and language choice.

Alternatively, Gwen could ask that every pupil transforms the original advertisement for two *new* audiences. This gives her means to see how closely each individual pupil has read the original text and how capable they are of transposing it to each new context. The juxtaposition of their examples will reveal how subtle their appreciation of audience is and their skill in tailoring language accordingly. If Gwen has any reservations about how convincingly these transformation exercises demonstrate pupils' reading ability, she could also conclude the scheme of work with a related assessment in the form of a commentary. Here pupils would provide a brief analysis of the moving image text, and then provide an explanation of the details they adapted or added as they reshaped the same message for a new context and new reader. In doing so, Gwen can guide them in identifying an item in the source text for change, to help them trace the shift in mode in their self-produced texts. They will need support to articulate with concise description the resources used initially (for example a particular camera shot), and then to pick out their uses of language in the transformed versions. These comments will be akin to conventional literary analysis, usually building explanations from quotations and highlighting how they have crafted phrases or selected words with a particular effect in mind.

Conclusion

Media education is invisible in the 2014 curriculum. Without knowledge of earlier versions of the English curriculum, it would be easy to assume by looking at the current version that the subject of English plays no part in educating young people in facets of contemporary media, especially where it involves moving images.

Gwen's lesson makes clear the relevance of the moving image. Where the curriculum directs your attention as a teacher of English to print-based texts, moving-image texts retain considerable potential to support analysis and to clarify how communication for various purposes can operate. Contrasting the same news story from radio or television with a newspaper or web version can help pupils see with greater clarity the significance of features particular to printed or verbal forms. The functioning of organisational conventions can become more visible, for example, or the selectivity of presentation of speech (direct or reported) more apparent if set aside a full radio interview. Working to other learning objectives based around purposes of communication, the use of television advertisements next to magazine advertisements could help pupils understand persuasion or, more subtly, the many ways in which advertisements aim to appeal to us and then manipulate our response. The potential of modern media texts to engage pupils is also clear, though perhaps that is just indicative of one way in which young people experience the world and why media education is important for its own sake, in English but also across the whole curriculum.

The advertisements

Incubate-innovation (2013) Ford Fiesta advertisement (http://incubate-innovation.org/2013/09/11/watch-rafael-rozendaals-ford-fiesta-advertisement/).
The Independent (2013) Galaxy Chocolate advertisement (http://www.independent.co.uk/arts-entertainment/tv/features/audrey-hepburn-advertise galaxy-chocolate-bars-over-her-dead-body-8508603.html).
Go Compare (2014) Bus Stop advertisement (http://www.gocompare.com/tv-advert/gio-compario-bares-his-soul-at-a-bus-stop/).

Websites

CHICAM: http://www.chicam.org
CivicWeb: http://civicweb.eu
The History of Advertising Trust: http://www.hatads.org.uk
Thinkbox: http://www.thinkbox.tv

References

Australian Curriculum, Assessment and Reporting Authority (2014) *Senior Secondary Curriculum: English*. Online at: http://www.australiancurriculum.edu.au/Senior Secondary/english/english/RationaleAims). (accessed 1 October 2014)
Buckingham, David (2000) *The Making of Citizens: Young People, News and Politics*. London: Routledge.
Buckingham, David (2003) *Media Education: Literacy, Learning and Contemporary Culture*. Cambridge: Polity Press.
Cazden, Courtney, Cope, Bill, Fairclough, Norman, Gee, Jim et al. (1996) 'A pedagogy of multiliteracies: designing social futures', *Harvard Educational Review*, 66 (1): 60–92.
CivicWeb (2007) *D4 Report: Young People, the Internet and Civic Participation: State of the Art Report*. London: Institute of Education.
Dahlgren, P. (2007a) *Media and Civic Engagement*. New York: Cambridge University Press.
Dahlgren, P. (ed.) (2007b) *Young Citizens and New Media: Learning for Democratic Participation*. London: Routledge.
Dahlgren, P. and Olsson, T. (2007) 'Facilitating political participation: young citizens, internet and civic cultures', in S. Livingstone and K. Drotner (eds), *The International Handbook of Children, Media and Culture*. London: Sage.
DCFS (2008) *Framework for Secondary English*. London: DCSF.
de Block, Liesbeth and Sefton-Green, Julian (2004) 'Refugee children in a virtual world: intercultural online communication and community', in A. J. Brown

and N. E. Davis (eds), *Digital Technology, Communities and Education: World Yearbook of Education*. London: RoutledgeFalmer, pp. 196–210.

DfE (2013) *English Programmes of Study: Key Stage 3 (National Curriculum in England)*. Reference: DFE-00184-2013.

DfE (2014) *English Programmes of Study: Key Stage 4 (National Curriculum in England)*. Reference: DFE-00497-2014.

DfEE (1999) *The National Curriculum*. London: DfEE/QCA.

Livingstone, Sonia and Bober, Magdalena (2005) *UK Children Go Online: Final Report of Key Project Findings 6*. London: London School of Economics and Political Science.

Morgan, Wendy (1997) *Critical Literacy in the Classroom: The Art of the Possible*. London: Routledge.

New Zealand Ministry of Education (2014) The New Zealand Curriculum; online at: http://nzcurriculum.tki.org.nz/The-New-Zealand-Curriculum/Learning-areas/English. (accessed 1 October 2014)

Ofsted (2013) *The Annual Report of Her Majesty's Chief Inspector of Education, Children's Services and Skills*. Norwich: TSO.

Ontario Ministry of Education (2007) *The Ontario Curriculum Grades 11 and 12, English (Revised)*; online at: http://www.edu.gov.on.ca/eng/curriculum/secondary/english1112currb.pdf. (accessed 1 October 2014)

CHAPTER 8

SPOKEN LANGUAGE

Objectives of this chapter:

- To explain the place of spoken language in the current curriculum
- To consider lesson design and its relationship with assessment of spoken language
- To advise on use of assessment criteria to inform lesson design and on presenting them to pupils
- To recognise the significance of pupils' understanding of the underlying purpose of their communication

---

Introduction: Marie's lesson

Marie teaches a lesson that is part of a unit for developing pupils' spoken language. She works with a Key Stage 4 group, building on pupils' experiences at Key Stage 3 to address the requirements of the curriculum. At Key Stage 3 the current requirements for Spoken Language recognise skills in this area as key to pupils' development 'cognitively, socially and linguistically' (DfE, 2013: 13). The curriculum also stresses that spoken language 'underpins the development of reading and writing':

> The quality and variety of language that pupils hear and speak are vital for developing their vocabulary and grammar and their understanding for reading and writing. Teachers should therefore ensure the continual development of pupils' confidence and competence in spoken language and listening skills.

Marie's lesson recognises the same connections as she engages her class in preparing persuasive speeches prior to pupils writing with the same purpose to persuade readers of a particular point of view.

In its comment on Spoken Language, the curriculum also sees the capacity of pupils to explain ideas verbally as a step towards fluency in writing. Its details apply this as much to their work around literature as they do to pupils 'making their thinking clear to themselves as well as to others'. In addition it states that teachers must guide their pupils 'to understand and use the conventions for discussion and debate'. Marie's lesson objectives complement these last items most directly, and in particular she identifies lesson objectives concerned with effective and persuasive speech making. These are:

- To know some techniques of persuasion and what makes an effective presentation
- To understand the different effects of these techniques on the speaker's audience
- To use the techniques and to develop an argument for their presentations

As a stimulus for their presentation, Marie uses the common and often effective strategy of using a genre familiar to pupils from television. The format of the programme *Room 101* is frequently used as a basis for individual pupil presentations as it has simplicity of purpose combined with content that derives from pupils' personal experience. They need only identify something they dislike, explain why and persuade their audience to relegate the object of their dislike to disposal in *Room 101*. The literary origin of the concept will be clear to teachers of English literature if not to their pupils. In George Orwell's *Nineteen Eighty-Four* (1949/1987) that room is where we meet our greatest fears, just as Winston is forced to confront his terror of rats.

Marie has to do more than engage and guide pupils in the nature of the format. She will also make an assessment of pupils' abilities in the area of Spoken Language, though the outcomes will not be aggregated within assessment scores that influence the final examination results pupils receive (changes in autumn 2013 removed the spoken language component from most English GCSEs). Her lesson then is primarily about spoken language skills, has a connection with writing, and makes demands on her own developing expertise and confidence in the area of assessment.

Marie's lesson plan

At this stage in her training (seven months into the nine-month programme), Marie is using a plan which is intended to prepare her for the quantity of lesson plans she will produce in her first post as a qualified teacher and the frequency with which she will prepare them too. The details on her plan are therefore relatively concise, showing the shape of the lesson. She is not required at this stage to record the detail of subtle aspects such as differentiation separately, but would be expected to be able to articulate them verbally and through reference to her resources. The lesson follows others where pupils were introduced to persuasive techniques in speeches, and is intended to prepare them for making individual presentations to peers in lessons to follow.

The sequence of her plan is presented in Figure 8.1. It shows activity details matched against estimates of the duration of each phase in a lesson of one hour in total. Marie used the AFOREST mnemonic to help pupils make use of these devices in their speech-making: alliteration, facts, opinions, rhetorical questions, emotive language, statistics and triplets (such as 'liberté, egalité, fraternité' or 'education, education, education').

Issues relevant to Marie's lesson

At a very early stage in her teaching career, Marie has to juggle many competing demands in a single lesson. On one hand she is trying to develop pupils' facility in spoken language, but on the other the process is also linked to writing. She is also trying to make assessments of pupils' speaking and listening activity, which can prove logistically complex for a teacher of English. All pupils will be making a presentation, but even if every pupil in a typical class of around thirty pupils were to speak for only a couple of minutes the assessments would take more than a full

Phase	Time	Activity
1	5	Pupils consider and record ideas for items they want to put in Room 101 – write two ideas on a Post-it note. Pupils in pairs: explain to partner one of their items.
2	5	Pupils put Post-it note on board. Teacher summarises for class and conducts quick survey of whether or not items merit sending to Room 101 – quick 'hands up' indication. Some questioning of individual pupils about why they want to send their items to Room 101.
3	5	Teacher explains sequence of lessons ahead: pupils will make their presentations, to be assessed against shared marking criteria. All pupils have the criteria for reference. Teacher explains marking criteria and gives pupils some time to read these independently too. Pupils (in pairs) asked to consider the traits of a high-scoring presentation. Plenary discussion of qualities of high-scoring presentation.
4	15	Teacher shows pupils video material (official examination board moderating example) of two individual presentations. Pupils asked to apply the marking criteria and decide which bands the presentations in the clips demonstrate. Plenary phase eliciting awarded bands from pupils and their explanations for their judgements.
5	15	Pupils asked to select just one of the items they want to send to Room 101. Pupils write a short paragraph using persuasive techniques following the AFOREST acronym (see text for explanation). All pupils required to include at least three techniques, but five if possible.
6	15	Pupils present their written speech to a partner, with the partner asked to assess according to the marking criteria. Partners should also provide advice for speakers on how to improve their speeches. Some examples to be shared with the whole class if time allows.

Figure 8.1 Marie's *Room 101*/spoken language assessment lesson plan

lesson to complete once time for introducing and changing from one speaker to the next is taken into account. Because the process of hearing each presentation will probably occupy at least two lessons and thus speeches will need to be of short duration, Marie needs to ensure pupils are very clear about the skills they need to demonstrate and how these link with the criteria. This means she has to guide them to be concise and to use a number of persuasive techniques concurrently. In the lesson described here she took steps to help them focus on significant assessment criteria. A symptom of this approach, however, is that the underlying purpose of persuasion can be obscured. It is also possible for audiences to be left unswayed by a speech that could contain several persuasive techniques, for their use does not guarantee their impact.

Assessment criteria that are broken up in this way can distract pupils from a holistic appreciation of persuasion. It can mean that the logic and coherence of an argument is overlooked, or that the potential of a topic to engage the emotions of an audience is left aside.

Marie's resources for the lesson (the video clips, the marking criteria) and the chosen format (*Room 101*) do not need changing for her to convey something of this more holistic conception of spoken language activity. She can maintain concentration on assessment criteria but at the same time draw out the persuasive dimension more fully. If she can achieve this, the concepts in the criteria will become more meaningful to pupils. The teacher's role here entails maintaining pupils' attention to effective communication, and mediating the criteria so they clarify the features of persuasive speech rather than drive the whole lesson. Without care to establish this balance, pupils could perceive the assessment as an end in itself rather than a means to gauge the quality of their communication generally. While Marie's instinct to use peer-assessment is sound because it involves pupils in evaluating the speeches of their partners, the approach she takes misses the opportunity for them to single out the features of a speech that led them to take one position or another. With the purpose of persuasion as the focus, the simplest evaluation has to be based on questions such as 'Did I persuade you to agree with me?' or 'Did you change your opinion based on what you heard in my speech?' The evaluation then looks to the impact of the speeches first, and only once the effectiveness of them has been identified can the relevance of discrete features have any significance.

Marie's tutor provides written comment on the lesson

Thanks Marie – a really useful lesson to see in terms of using assessment criteria and 'assessment for learning' techniques. The lesson confirmed your skills in providing clear and concise instructions and showed that you can guide activities with good pace and focus. Your questioning was often successful, involving many pupils and making good use of follow-up questions.

The materials you presented were all useful and pupils made progress in understanding the details of the assessment criteria. In your question-and-answer phase, you helpfully asked pupils to put some of the criteria detail into their own words. When they spoke about the strand concerning the structure of a presentation, they summed this up as 'getting to the point'. The significance of some of the details in the criteria points to a strategy to help pupils make effective presentations. You could ask them to identify three key points about their *Room 101* items, and to treat these like topic sentences in writing. The things they select can act as signposts for their speeches and give them a simple means to lend structure to what they say.

Using video examples provided by the exam board serves to give pupils a sense of what presentations can look like, and provides a clear focus for applying the criteria. Using two clips also helps signal a range of attainment and differing uses of the criteria. Because you want pupils to make progress in terms of the skill of persuasion, try to make sure there is opportunity in the lesson for them to experience the effects of persuasion before getting to the assessment criteria. Naturally there may not be more time available for a new or different activity, but you could manipulate the clips differently. You could use the first presentation example, or even just a part of it, as a focus for pupils to reflect on persuasion. To what extent did the speaker persuade them of their argument? If pupils concentrate on this first, they are likely to understand the criteria they apply to the next one more fully. The match between the criteria and the effectiveness of a speech in terms of communication becomes clearer.

It is also challenging for pupils to apply complex criteria well when the details cover so many things. Perhaps separate the terms of the criteria for pupils and give different groups of pupils (for example rows) a different focus each. This means they can really concentrate on what their own criterion means in terms of the video and balances the challenge of watching the clip for the first time with thinking about it in terms of the criteria. An alternative is for you to plan to use the clips section by section, pausing at key moments and asking the whole class to focus on different criteria at each stage.

In discussion, the tutor and Marie also considered the degree to which the lesson activity matched the declared objectives and their consistent emphasis on persuasion. It would be hard for Marie to assert that pupils had actually made progress in respect to those, despite the relevance of each to the criteria.

Helping Marie clarify the purpose of her lesson

One thing to keep in mind about Marie's lesson is its usefulness. The process of familiarising pupils with success criteria in this way is consistent with the principles of Assessment for Learning, first outlined by Black and Wiliam (1990) and revisited in many government-led initiatives since. An influential document from 2002 (Assessment Reform Group, 2002), for instance, identified 'promoting understanding of goals and criteria' as one of its ten principles, stating 'assessment for learning should promote commitment to learning goals and a shared understanding of the criteria by which they are assessed'. It offered further detail:

> For effective learning to take place learners need to understand what it is they are trying to achieve – and want to achieve it. Understanding and commitment follows when learners have some part in deciding goals and identifying criteria for assessing progress. Communicating assessment criteria involves discussing them with learners using terms that they can understand, providing examples of how the criteria can be met in practice and engaging learners in peer- and self-assessment.

Marie's lesson does identify and clarify the relevant criteria, and she provides space for pupils to articulate them in their own terms. She shows them presentations on video and asks them to apply the criteria, and she incorporates peer-assessment. She also goes some way to support their understanding of the goal, that is to persuade listeners of a point of view.

Having taught and then discussed the lesson with her tutor, Marie soon acknowledged scope to attend to this goal of the lesson more thoroughly. She felt the goal of persuasion needed more explanation so that pupils could link it with the criteria more readily and in particular have in mind the matter of persuasive impact on listeners. Her own understanding of assessment for learning moved on, so that she would not only work through the recognisable principles of the process but also see that when applied they need to merge with the particular demands of this English task and the qualities of effective communication. In her development as a teacher this entails looking more closely at the minutiae of assessment criteria and teasing out the implications of often quite broad and generalised statements relative to the immediate topic.

Before the lesson Marie looked closely at band descriptors for this area of assessment and paraphrased them for pupils. In particular she drew on descriptors associated with the skills of 'communicating and adapting language' rather than the strands about 'interacting and responding' or 'creating and sustaining roles'. At the highest levels of attainment ('sophisticated and impressive') these focus on communicating complex and demanding subject matter, using a wide repertoire of strategies suited to the communication purpose and assured use of Standard English and vocabulary. The lowest band descriptors likewise focus on the content (brief expression of points of view, ideas and feelings), making apt use of non-verbal modes of presentation and basic features of Standard English. The influence of these items is evident in Marie's use of the AFOREST acronym to help her pupils use a repertoire of persuasive techniques consistent with the higher band descriptor requirements around speech content. In addressing these, then, Marie is making informed and constructive decisions that can contribute to the success of her pupils in the task. The lesson plan, her handling of the criteria during teaching and her comments about them afterwards combine to confirm that she has already established a good level of teacherly knowledge about the assessment framework.

The aspect Marie wants to refine is how well she can synthesise this information with helping pupils understand the purpose of this communication – to persuade others. In a way she has done much of the difficult work, having dealt with niggling aspects that benefit from pedantic attention to detail. By scrutinising the band descriptors, however, she overlooked the statements underpinning the specification guidance for Spoken Language. These took the form of assessment objectives (Ofqual, 2011: 4) common to all examination boards, and highlight the most significant objectives to be addressed, whichever one of the three strands Marie or any teacher elects as the most relevant. The four objectives are these:

1. Speak to communicate clearly and purposefully; structure and sustain talk, adapting it to different situations and audiences; use standard English and a variety of techniques as appropriate.
2. Listen and respond to speakers' ideas, perspectives and how they construct and express their meanings.
3. Interact with others, shaping meanings through suggestions, comments and questions and drawing ideas together.
4. Create and sustain different roles.

Marie's unit addresses the first objective as the one most relevant to individual presentations by pupils, though there is opportunity in her lesson structure to address the second consistent with the peer-assessment mechanisms she includes. Marie did address some elements of the first objective, especially the last detail about techniques. The responses of pupils during the lesson, as they paraphrased criteria as 'getting to the point', show how Marie's teaching also prompted thought around 'structure and sustain talk'.

The items enjoying less emphasis were the one about communicating 'purposefully' and the linked matter of adapting speech for 'situations and audiences'. It would be wrong to say these weren't touched upon during Marie's lesson, but if you look at her lesson plan you can see that at no point are either dealt with overtly, despite her lesson objectives declaring persuasion as the core. As a consequence their treatment then can only be incidental, a matter of chance rather than an essential and founding consideration in pupils' preparation to give an effective persuasive speech with impact on their audience.

It's interesting if we look at the lesson objectives again that Marie does have her second objective formulated around audience – indeed it is very well phrased:

- To know some techniques of persuasion and what makes an effective presentation
- *To understand the different effects of these techniques on the speaker's audience*
- To use the techniques and to develop an argument for their presentation.

Unfortunately the lesson activities don't address the effects on the audience very thoroughly, though we can imagine that discussion of the audience might be tacit. If Marie were to modify phases 4, 5 and 6 of her lesson just slightly she could address the audience more successfully. First, she can manipulate the video material in phase 4, so that she asks pupils directly whether or not they were persuaded to take the position of speakers. If yes, can her pupils identify two or three aspects that swayed them? If not, what else would the video examples need to include? She could also exploit the simple fact of the juxtaposition of the two clips. Of the two, which do pupils find most persuasive and why? Because Marie's objective declares her intention that pupils will *understand* the various effects of the techniques used, she also needs to devote some time to demonstrating the use of the techniques and, additionally, giving pupils the opportunity to describe their effects. This is the point where she needs to prepare her video material with deliberation. When she comes to teach, this would make phase 4 a little longer but should ensure it has a greater effect on outcomes in phases 5 and 6.

First, she should ask herself what different techniques are demonstrated in the examples? Second, for each technique exemplified, what vocabulary will her pupils need to describe the range of possible effects? Further, are there a couple of instances within the material of the same technique being used but to potentially very different effect? Note that the words 'possible' and 'potential' are used here, because Marie can't know for sure how pupils will react and what the actual effect of the examples will be. She needs to keep hold of this if she is going to do justice to the persuasive power of these presentations as something real, something that actually works on her pupils as listeners. Nevertheless, Marie will be able to anticipate a range of possible effects and perhaps be able to surmise the speaker's intention too, regardless of the presenter's level of success. Marie will be able to generate vocabulary and sentence stems that help pupils discuss the effect of the examples. They could include terms like these:

> The rhetorical question makes me think about …
> The rhetorical question suggests the speaker's position is …
> The image the speaker uses makes me feel …
> The words which manipulate my emotions most are … because …
> The most persuasive detail for me is …
> The speech emphasises x over y, and therefore makes me believe …

As well as these stems pupils may need to refer to a word bank that describes differing and contrasting emotions, but which needs to go beyond the terms *happy* and *sad* to accommodate nuance. There may be expressions used to prey on insecurities, to prompt laughter or to provoke rage and pupils will need a vocabulary to capture those effects. Pupils will also need vocabulary that allows them to express evaluative comment, so that they can say whether they are 'entirely convinced' or if, instead, they are merely left to 'reconsider' their position. The extent to which they may be persuaded will vary and this matter of degree is something for them to take into account with their own presentations. When it comes to peer-evaluation in phase 6, that first step question 'Was I persuaded?' could be nuanced in forms such as 'To what extent was I persuaded?' and a scale or continuum of options might help pupils visualise their level of impact.

Phase 5 of Marie's lesson would also need adjustment following the improved attention to effects in phase 4. This phase is a chance to address effects further as well. Instead of asking pupils to draft a speech including three to five instances of persuasive technique, Marie could rethink the preparation so that it is less about the number of persuasive devices used. She might only ask pupils to use two techniques, and introduce a level of challenge not through quantity but through attention to the impact of the techniques used. Rather than write a paragraph, pupils could draft two persuasive statements across the first five minutes of the phase, and then in the next five make a brief note of the intended effect of each. This asks them to be self-conscious and constitutes metacognition, the process of becoming self-aware about one's thought process and communicative intent. If sentence stems like those above are introduced in this part of the lesson, the speech-maker could choose the ones most relevant to their speech as prompts for response by their peers. Phase 6 now allows them to judge the effectiveness of their statements according to their intention, seeing if the comment and responses of their peers match their intentions. The phase could be shorter but have increased focus and a revised function of directing pupils' attention to effects consistent with the lesson objectives. Once pupils have considered effect with this level of deliberation, pupils can write the rest of their speech and then apply the formal assessment criteria as the final stage of the lesson. None of these changes requires Marie to redesign her lesson because she was working to sound principles in her original version. They are just about a shift in emphasis that allows her to fulfil her declared objectives more directly.

Conclusion: some wider purposes of Spoken Language work

Marie's lesson has the merits of paying attention to the requirements of the relevant examination specification in both planning and assessment. Because she recognises the importance of particular assessment criteria, she also makes a sensible decision to make pupils aware of these and to help them understand what constitutes success relative to each. The details of the examination specification exert significant influence on her work as they do for most teachers, as does the responsibility for ensuring her class achieves well relative to this framework.

In terms of her developing thought about spoken language activity, however, it would be useful for Marie to return to that phrase in the curriculum that suggests a holistic view of learning in this area. It referred to the influence of the role of spoken language in supporting pupils' development 'cognitively, socially and linguistically' (DfE, 2013: 13). That combination has strong echoes of a social-constructivist view of language development, which asserts the importance of social interaction through dialogue in the process of concept formation and understanding for individuals. This view of learning argues that discussion between individuals permits the exploration of ideas, sharing provisional thoughts that can become clearer and more refined through the contribution of others. By vocalising thoughts and hearing how others respond, we clarify the verbal expression of ideas for ourselves and in our own minds (see Vygotsky, 1986).

This view of language is one that Marie could bring to much of her English teaching, and not just that which concerns Spoken Language as an overt domain of the curriculum and as a strand of pupil activity. Similar principles are articulated in recent surveys of practice such as *Removing Barriers to Literacy* (Ofsted, 2011) and have been present in guidance for many years. A report from 2003, *Yes He Can: Schools Where Boys Write Well* (also Ofsted), promoted the verbal preparation of ideas between pupils before they put pen to page.

More broadly, and in independent research, Robin Alexander has been influential in describing the benefits of 'dialogic talk' (Alexander, 2008) as a basis for fostering independence and confidence in pupils. A similar interest is evident in the work of the Thinking Together project headed by Neil Mercer and associated publications (see Littleton and Mercer, 2013).

Though Marie works in a context where imperatives are defined by the immediate demands of the curriculum or the examination board's specifications, she also has a wider view of her work and a commitment to preparing her pupils for life beyond school and outside the realm of formal assessment and qualifications. She will be developing the articulacy of all her pupils and for some will be addressing significant Speech, Language and Communication Needs (National Children's Bureau, 2013). Her success in these will impact on the life opportunities and enfranchisement (or otherwise) of her pupils, but clearly it cannot be her responsibility alone. It will be the work not only of her department, but of the school and its community. At the same time that cannot be divorced from the influences of the wider world.

It might be apt to give some attention to the pros and cons of using popular culture formats for pupils too. *Room 101* has many practical benefits, not least the level of engagement it promotes, but given its interest in items to be dismissed it may not provide a model of communication for constructive purposes. Further, its format is an abstraction insofar it exists only in the world of television, a form of negative wish-fulfilment that has no parallel in the real world. The ability to dispose so easily of the things we dislike is not replicated in day-to-day interaction, even if the capacity to articulate an opinion may be.

References

Alexander, Robin J. (2008) *Towards Dialogic Teaching: Rethinking Classroom Talk*, 4th edn. York: Dialogos.

Assessment Reform Group (2002) *Assessment for Learning: 10 Principles*. University of Cambridge School of Education, Assessment Reform Group.

Black, Paul and Wiliam, Dylan (1990) *Inside the Black Box*. London: GL Assessment.

DfE (2013) *English Programmes of Study: Key Stage 3 (National Curriculum in England)*. Reference: DFE-00184-2013.

Littleton, Karen and Mercer, Neil (2013) *Interthinking: Putting Talk to Work*. Abingdon: Routledge.

National Children's Bureau/Early Support (2013) *Information About Speech, Language and Communication Needs*, 2nd edn. Richmond: Office of Public Sector Information.

Ofqual (2011) *GCSE Subject Criteria for English*. Coventry: Ofqual.

Ofsted (2003) *Yes He Can: Schools Where Boys Write Well*. London: HMI.

Ofsted (2011) *Removing Barriers to Literacy*. London: HMI.

Orwell, George (1949) *Nineteen Eighty-Four*. London: Penguin.

Vygotsky, Lev S. (1986) *Thought and Language*. Cambridge, MA: MIT Press.

CHAPTER 9

TEACHING SHAKESPEARE

Objectives of this chapter:

- To approach teaching Shakespeare plays as drama, giving pupils the means to comment on aspects of stagecraft and dramatic effects
- To introduce and apply to lesson design active methods of the type devised by Rex Gibson
- To explore the phenomenon of tension in a scene, and how to support pupils to recognise it and to express in writing how it functions to affect an audience

Introduction

This chapter looks at working with Shakespeare's plays, with Ollie's lesson on *Henry V* as the focus for discussion. His objectives concern how tension builds in the scene, and it is this aspect which is likely to be of most interest if you are thinking about applying the principles outlined here to other plays. The instances of dramatic tension in Shakespeare's plays are many, so inevitably you will find yourself guiding pupils in an exploration of tension at every level, from Key Stage 3 classes through to A-level. Shakespeare is central to the Reading programme of study in the National Curriculum (DfE, 2013) and A-level specifications always include a unit based on his work. Tension is something that can prove difficult to teach but a few pointers can help you avoid common pitfalls so that pupils build confidence with it quickly.

Ollie is looking at Act 2, scene 2 with his pupils. If you are unfamiliar with the play, it is important to know that Henry is making preparations for war with France. He has learned that three of his closest advisors have betrayed him and is set to confront them about their treason. He does not do so immediately, a point crucial to increasing tension in the scene.

Ollie uses this abridged version:

[Enter EXETER, BEDFORD, and WESTMORELAND]

BEDFORD	'Fore God, his grace is bold, to trust these traitors.
WESTMORELAND	How smooth and even they do bear themselves!
	As if allegiance in their bosoms sat.
EXETER	That man was his bedfellow,
	– That he should, for a foreign purse, so sell
	His sovereign's life!

[Trumpets sound. Enter KING HENRY V, SCROOP, CAMBRIDGE, GREY, and Attendants]

HENRY	Now sits the wind fair, and we will aboard.
	My Lord of Cambridge, and my kind Lord of
	Masham, my gentle knight, give me your thoughts.
	Think you not that the powers we bear
	Will cut through the force of France?
SCROOP	No doubt, my liege, if each man do his best.
CAMBRIDGE	Never was monarch better fear'd and loved
	Than is your majesty.
GREY	True: your father's enemies do serve you
	With hearts create of duty and of zeal.
HENRY	Uncle of Exeter, enlarge the man committed
	Yesterday, that rail'd against our person: we pardon
	him.
SCROOP	That's mercy, but too much security:
	Let him be punish'd, sovereign.
HENRY	O, let us yet be merciful.
CAMBRIDGE	So may your highness, and yet punish too.

GREY	You show great mercy, if you give him life.
HENRY	If little faults, shall not be wink'd at, how shall we stretch our eye when capital crimes appear before us? And now to our French causes …

[Henry hands over the papers to CAMBRIDGE, GREY and SCROOP]

HENRY	Read them; and know, I know your worthiness. Why, how now, gentlemen?

It is possible that as you read this extract you may be confused about who Henry addresses at each turn, and the potential confusion is there in the unabridged scene too. There is variation between names Henry uses in dialogue and those in the script and stage directions. The king calls the character of Scroop 'Lord Masham' (line 13) and Grey 'my gentle knight' (line 14). Being clear about the direction of address is crucial if pupils are to understand which character Henry confronts in turn with summary of their guilt (lines 76–141) prior to their arrest. Before Ollie can begin to address tension, then, there are fundamental matters of comprehension to consider too.

Ollie's lesson

Ollie's lesson is well-structured, with stages designed carefully to anticipate pupils' possible difficulties with the scene and to engage them as fully as possible. The key steps in the lesson are as follows:

Ollie explains that Henry has learned of a plot against him and is about to meet with them.

He asks pupils to predict what might happen, discussing in pairs ready to share thoughts in a whole-class discussion afterwards.

Ollie shows pupils an adaptation of the scene from Kenneth Branagh's film of the play and indicates that as they watch they should look closely at the emotions of characters and how tension builds.

Ollie allocates pupils in groups and provides them with copies of the abridged scene in print. He asks each group to select three key moments that show the increasing tension, highlighting relevant details. Each pupil makes a record of the chosen quotations in a table format.

(Continued)

(Continued)

Working individually, pupils make notes on each quotation remarking on what they tell us about each character's emotions and on any interesting features of language, including identification of literary devices.

Ollie follows this with a plenary phase based around two questions: *How does Shakespeare's language build tension? What do we learn about the characters' emotions?*

To conclude, Ollie asks pupils to select one quotation from their table and with the help of their notes to write a point-evidence-explain paragraph explaining how effective it is in building tension.

The lesson concludes with three pupils reading their writing aloud to the rest of the group. The examples explain what the quotations mean confidently enough, but not one of them provides a really convincing explanation of how tension builds.

Comment on Ollie's lesson

Before Ollie's lesson is considered at length, here are some of the comments he received in written feedback after teaching. As you might expect, the notes were elaborated verbally too.

Your idea of asking pupils to select key moments is a sensible one. I recommend you try to support this even more deliberately. Before pupils select moments establish (a) the starting point – the state of equilibrium, and (b) the climax following the building tension. The crux of identifying tension is to recognise incremental steps – how one builds on the next, the shifts that come step-by-step. Sometimes analogies help here: it could be likened to shifting gear, perhaps.

In some cases it can help to identify techniques or features that create tension too, for instance directly contradictory statements by characters, something happening on stage that one character is not aware of, an increase in movement … This approach might help you address the emotional aspect and perhaps articulate a formula that helps pupils understand the interplay of the different components, possibly 'tension = changing events + heightened emotion'. The important thing is to integrate emotion into pupils' understanding of tension.

The comments suggest an even more precise approach to framing pupils' understanding of tension. Pupils may well be very used to commenting about literature using an approach to paragraphing such as the point-evidence-explain pattern, but the development of tension cannot be explained easily within that structure. Ollie's lesson guided pupils to consider relevant textual detail, and took steps to help pupils understand the action of the scene as well as the words, but he had room to frame tension more conspicuously for them.

Working backwards from the lesson outcomes, we can see that though pupils wrote decent paragraphs making use of quotation, these tended to confirm their ability to use quotation rather than support their progress in expressing how the scene builds tension for the audience. If we think about the concept of tension, something that unfolds over time, the formula of point-evidence-explain isn't likely to support sophisticated comment about it. Invariably the evidence in such writing tends to be an isolated quotation, divorced from context. Inherent in the idea of tension, conversely, is the notion of change. There has to be, or it couldn't build. Some of Ollie's pupils selected the quotation 'Read them; and know, I know your worthiness' as a focus for comment, and reasonably so as it is a very relevant quotation. The problem is that its impact can't easily be explained if it is presented alone. It needs a counterpoint if a build-up of tension is to be traced. This is exactly what the feedback means when it talks about the movement from equilibrium to climax. This raises two pedagogical considerations for the teacher. The first concerns scaffolding (see Bruner (1966) for the introduction of this term) the lesson so that pupils work in a framework that makes this sort of movement overt, and the second is about thinking through the writing demands of expressing the shift (see, for example, Andrews (2008) and Lewis and Wray (1996) on the particular demands of different writing tasks). What vocabulary can contribute to clear explanation? Further, what sort of paragraph structure is needed? It is likely it will have to draw on at least two instances of textual detail if it is to adequately serve its purpose of explaining the creation and intensification of tension.

The second line of discussion responds to Ollie's interest in emotions in the scene and how these relate to tension. It is an important strand, suggesting a holistic approach to the text which balances attention to the script as a blueprint for drama with treatment of it as an object for literary analysis. In terms of the scene, it demonstrates Ollie's alertness to what might lie between the lines and thus to the unstated possibilities for action, in expression, gesture or movement. When Henry asks 'Why, how now, gentlemen?' it doesn't follow directly from the previous line. Something must happen in-between, unvoiced but apparent to the king and presumably the audience. So Ollie's approach acknowledges performance and recognises that pupils need to understand it to inform their analysis.

Classroom treatment of tension has to marry that clarity of what it means to explain it with what it means in action on stage. If Ollie can make this connection more strongly he is likely to realise the potential of his lesson more fully.

Creating a framework for considering tension

The first thing Ollie needs to do to support his pupils' understanding of tension is to point out for them the start and end points, in this case the initial state of relative equilibrium and the climax. Usefully, Shakespeare himself gives us vocabulary that complements this idea of balance, as the traitors are described by Westmoreland as 'smooth and even' in their bearing. It is this outward appearance, one of integrity and composure, that is undermined in the scene, as we learn that Henry sees through them and see ourselves that he confronts them. Because Ollie wants his pupils to write clearly about change from this early balance, it makes sense for him to describe the narrative arc of the extract from beginning to end. He might present to them something along these lines:

> *Shakespeare builds tension towards Henry confronting the traitors about their guilt. The extract starts with Bedford describing Henry's calm treatment of them: he is 'bold, to trust these'. By the end, however, Henry shows that he does not trust them. Instead, he shows them that he knows they have betrayed him. We know they are surprised when he confronts them with their guilt as he asks 'Why, how now gentlemen?'.*

The purpose of writing like this is to articulate clearly for pupils the movement of the scene, to give them a summary on which to reflect and build. It gives opportunity for revisiting and for reflection, capturing details they need to hold on to as an additional support to verbal discussion. It also offers an example of how to trace change by using two items of evidence drawn from the text, not just the typical isolated quotation of most point-evidence-explain paragraphs. To set them off from here Ollie might add that in today's lesson '… we will explain what happens in-between to build tension as the scene moves to the moment of accusation'. Everything that follows from this in the lesson is intended to gently support pupils' reading and interpretation of the text in preparation for organised and conceptualised writing, using paragraph and sentence constructions suited to describing and analysing distinctive features. It is a process that Deborah Fones has called 'blocking them in to free them to act' (Fones, 1999).

The next judgement for Ollie to make is how to help his pupils recognise how steps in the extract build towards tension. He could of course leave this entirely open, asking pupils to identify steps themselves. Alternatively, he may feel that some more overt structuring is necessary. This could be more efficient too with respect to the learning objectives focused on explaining how tension is created: he may not wish to lose valuable lesson time asking pupils to find the stages when some may not easily identify sections that serve them well for the focus skill of explanation. Here are four stages that could provide a framework for discussion. These do not represent a definitive way in which to separate the extract into sections, but they do indicate the potential of framing the extract in this way.

The fact that the arrangement falls into four is useful in the classroom. It is a division of the extract that avoids over-complexity for pupils while maintaining variation of sections sufficient to demonstrate development. Further, it is a convenient division for attention in groups, where one or even two teams could be designated a section each for close work before joining together. The proposed sections are these, complete with a suggested label that can consolidate pupils' sense of what happens in each section:

- The first section, from Bedford's ''Fore God …' to Exeter's 'His sovereign's life!' could be labelled 'Loyalty and treachery', to underline the distinction between these loyal servants (including Westmoreland too) and the three traitors who enter with the king. This exchange establishes for the audience their treasonable conduct and so gives the context for what follows. It signals in addition Henry's calm handling of this situation ('his grace is bold').
- A second section begins with the fanfare as 'trumpets sound' and Henry and the traitors enter. Henry addresses them as if nothing is amiss, asking what they think of England's prospects against France. It is very much a scene of keeping up appearances, so 'Appearances' seems a valid label. Just as Henry remains polite ('my kind Lord', 'my gentle knight'), Scroop, Cambridge and Grey respond with compliments for the king. The section concludes with Grey going so far as to point out that Henry has managed to secure the support even of those that were his 'father's enemies'. Each of the lords has had his turn to make an obsequious remark and thus the audience gets the measure of them.

- The third section, 'The Trap', starts with Henry taking the exchange in another direction with an aside to Exeter. By announcing he will pardon the man who 'rail'd' against him he lures the devious traitors to denounce the offender. They do, of course, each again taking their turn to discourage Henry from showing any mercy. A rhetorical question concludes this section, as Henry wonders aloud what punishments could match 'capital crimes' if even trivial misdemeanours attract such harsh sentencing as the three suggest.
- The final section is the shortest on the page, and can be called 'Guilty' to signpost the nature of the action. The accusation is tacit, and therein lies the interest in its presentation. The audience sees Henry hand over the papers personally. It is only through understanding his use of irony, and then seeing (or visualising) the response of the traitors in expression and gesture, that the audience can imagine what might be written on the documents.

Dividing in this way allows Ollie to present to pupils the components that contribute to tension, which is not the same as explaining it for them. Loyalty and Treachery, Appearances, The Trap and Guilty are labels giving simple means for pupils to grasp the key shifts in focus across the scene, and use straightforward descriptive vocabulary to aid comprehension and recall. The length of each section means that they are well-suited to close analysis around a single prompt. If Ollie wishes, he could give different groups or individuals one of the sections to comment on, using the label as a prompt to assist interpretation: 'You have an extract from the scene and you have a label. What links can you suggest between the two?' In this way he can maintain space for pupils to do their interpretive work, the chosen cue likely to encourage careful scrutiny of the details, line by line.

Once every pupil has considered at least one extract closely (whether individually or in a group), Ollie has numerous choices about how to support progress in learning. He could take the lesson forward by further exploiting a group arrangement, arranging new groups for discussions that help pupils see how each section has a different function and the changes from one to the next. This can be very easy, for example asking pupils who studied section one (group A) to work with those who studied section two (group B), paralleled by a group comprising those who looked at three (group C) and four (group D). A stimulus question here could concentrate on the information provided for the audience: What information does each section give the audience and how are they different? A worthwhile extension of this could be to then match up section two experts with those for three (groups B and C) so that pupils see a different development. That leaves group A to work with group D, meaning that pupils here can have a perspective that spans the whole extract, though the prompt about information and difference still applies. It wouldn't be essential, and may even be too repetitive, but it may be justified to have a third stage, so that by the end each group works with their counterpart experts for each of the other sections (see Sage (2000) for a discussion of group activities and Mercer (2000) for the rationale).

But Ollie may not want to orchestrate a sequence of group work. He might just as well ask pupils who have studied each section to report, in turn and in a whole-class setting, on their part of the extract. This gives Ollie scope to question pupils, add comment and provide or elicit further depth of analysis, and could provide opportunity too to verbalise vocabulary suited to describing the traits of characters (loyal, treacherous, cunning), the tone of comment (astounded, fawning, understated) and features of language (hyperbole, irony, rhetorical question) that give pupils the resources to describe the *language* that conveys to us the detail of action on stage.

The language pupils need is more than a matter of individual words. Whatever mechanism Ollie decides to use to afford sharing information on sections of the extract, it will help pupils too if there can be attention in the lesson to the extract beyond sentence level. This means following up the initial summary of the extract's narrative arc with time to identify and use phrases that also support explanation of the shifts between sections. These may arise spontaneously as pupils report, and in such moments Ollie's task is to capture them and draw attention to them, perhaps by recording them on the board and pointing out features of their construction. On the other hand he may opt for very deliberate treatment of relevant constructions, precisely because the demands of describing how tension is built across the piece differ so much from what conventional point-evidence-explain commentary permits. It could be useful, for example, to guide pupils in writing a paragraph to follow his introductory example, which summarises the steps in the scene:

> *Shakespeare gives the audience information little by little, so they can understand how dishonest these traitors are and see Henry's cunning. First, we see that Bedford, Exeter and Westmoreland are loyal to Henry as they describe 'these traitors', who have sided with France. Second …*

It is commentary that needs embedded quotation to anchor it to the text, and some skill in précis to describe concisely the development presented across the extract. Regardless of how many steps are identified or how they are arrived at, a construction that is stepped itself does such work: *First* or *To begin with*, *Second*, *Then* and *Finally* … The challenge is for pupils to sum up each stage in one sentence. From there, analysis can focus on how tension is created through quick or abrupt shifts in the action where pupils will need vocabulary and constructions to describe contrast or variation. The first example of a change is between the intimate, concerned exchange of the loyal lords to the grand entrance of Henry, attendants and traitors. It may be enough to mark the distinction between *private* dialogue and a *public* exchange (the fanfare proclaims it) and return to the interest in appearances. The *private/public* distinction is one easily generalised to other plays, as would juxtapositions such as *intimate/shared* and *secret/open*. The pedagogical principle of capturing the contrast is one that pupils can extend once they have seen examples. Finding the right words to express the turns in a scene from one moment to the next can be an aid to planning writing, with pupils considering and capturing the shifts concisely before starting extended writing. Paragraphs that articulate these developments probably need topic sentences that use the vocabulary of the contrast, for example: *Early in the scene we see an abrupt change from the private conversation between the loyal lords to the arrival of Henry and the traitors, marked very publicly with a fanfare.*

These approaches acknowledge the demands of writing about the structural dimension of tension, but as Ollie's original lesson identified, emotion is key too. These techniques for framing interpretation of the scene can't support a full response unless they are tied to close attention to the lines and the spaces in-between. For that, Ollie can do more to recognise the script as a stimulus for performance and for interpretation.

Understanding emotion through active methods

Ollie's lesson recognised that seeing an interpretation of this scene would support pupils in recognising tension. The Branagh version presents this part of the play so that building tension is very apparent. As quite a lengthy sequence it also demonstrates the room around the text, making clear to pupils the need to consider what goes on between and around the dialogue.

Ollie could exploit what he recognises as the qualities of the film version to guide his work with his pupils. As film, it emphasises gesture and facial expression as means to communicate the emotions and interaction of characters, and uses an abridged script akin to Ollie's own. Ollie can draw into his teaching the 'active methods' of teaching Shakespeare championed by Rex Gibson (1998: xii), which 'comprise a wide range of expressive, creative and physical activities' recognising that the plays were written for performance and benefit from enactment to support pupils' own intellectual and emotional engagement. Activity of this type 'gives focus and substance to the discussion, writing and design work that students undertake'. An interesting assertion by Gibson in the light of those observation notes Ollie received is that active methods 'dissolve the traditional oppositions of analysis and imagination, intellect and emotion'. Ollie recognised the importance of emotion in the scene but had difficulty addressing it so that it could inform pupils' appreciation and discussion of building tension. He might try an approach influenced by what is widely known as 'forum theatre', which derived from the work of Augusto Boal (2008). Forum theatre is a process that allows the audience to become directors, deciding and explaining to actors how they should perform. As a pedagogical approach to drama in education, it is often organised so that some pupils are positioned in the classroom space as performers, with others explaining to them where they should stand, how they should speak and so on. It can even involve those pupils in the audience replacing the performers to show their peers how they believe characters should be presented. The activity here was designed for pupils to work on in groups rather than as a whole class, but could be amended for a whole-class approach if preferred. It helps pupils reflect on what happens *around* the dialogue, to get at the hidden, unspoken aspects of the text that are nevertheless signalled in the script.

The aspects of performance pupils are asked to consider include:

- the interaction of characters;
- the position and movement of characters on the stage, including their entry and exit points;
- the gestures and facial expressions of characters;
- the intonation and emphasis characters place on their speech;
- the use of props.

In addition, the task requires pupils to think about pace and how a director might set about realising dramatic tension in performance. In introducing such activity to pupils it helps to emphasise the fact that the impact of scenes in terms of likely audience reaction is not always evident on the page, and that relatively short extracts may be substantial in terms of performance time. This is especially true of this extract from *Henry V* and of special relevance to the fourth and final section we identified. One significant aspect of this short extract is that once the choreography and silences are worked into performance the scene may be quite lengthy in duration, as the Branagh version confirms.

Setting up this forum theatre work is quite simple, though the level of direction and supervision can vary depending on the class working on it. It is sensible for everyone to read the scene through individually first, as the group work is likely to be more purposeful and thoughtful if each pupil has some basic familiarity with the script. The next step is to allocate pupils to play the parts of characters, noting in this case that there are eight roles even allowing for just one attendant. It is probable that in a class of between 25 and 30 you could opt for either two large groups or three groups of about ten pupils: it is sensible to have performers for all the parts with at least a couple acting in a directing capacity to begin with.

The groups should be tasked with preparing the scene for performance, but keep the emphasis on working out the terms of the action consistent with the prompts above. The aim is not to arrive at a polished performance or beautiful reading of the words in the script. Instead, this is a form of problem-solving. This extract provides an excellent stimulus because pupils have to think very carefully to work out how they would like to direct the entrance of characters, their movement, to whom they address their speech, their expressions and gestures. If they are to speculate on what might be viable actions according to each category, pupils must scrutinise the script and the words attributed to each character.

It helps to define for pupils an area that will provide the stage so they can consider how characters will be positioned relative to the audience, and to provide them with a list of the bullet points above so they keep each element in mind. Ask pupils to build up their performance through a forum theatre-style approach: those in the director role can intervene to suggest to their actors alternative intonation, movement, gesture or positioning. In some cases the acting roles will be fluid as pupils switch to demonstrate these various ways of presenting the script.

It follows that this approach gives pupils a format by which to consider the emotions of characters in the scene, arising from discussion about how players orient to each other, their tone of voice and their expression. The opportunities can be demonstrated with attention to the last few lines of the extract, as Henry finally confronts the traitors with their guilt:

> If little faults, shall not be wink'd at, how shall we
> stretch our eye when capital crimes appear before
> us? And now to our French causes …

[Henry hands over the papers to CAMBRIDGE, GREY and SCROOP]

Read them; and know, I know your worthiness.
Why, how now, gentlemen?

Where does Henry direct his gaze as he makes his comment about punishments? Is it towards his loyal lords, perhaps with a knowing wink, or does he relish the irony and look towards Grey? And what of his tone of voice? It could be playful, or menacing, or anywhere in-between. The stage direction invites thought about the relative positions and stance of characters, with the possibility that the traitors appear eager for battle as they sustain their facade of loyalty and commitment. What does Henry do as he hands over the papers, and how long does it take between the traitors taking them and the king's next utterance? Presumably there needs to be sufficient time to convince the audience that Scroop, Cambridge and Grey have indeed read the papers, a moment of horrified comprehension and then a response to the death warrants they hold in their hands. What do the actors need to do between 'worthiness' and 'why'?

Because even this, the shortest of the sections, has so much to consider in terms of performance, the teacher may feel it offers sufficient challenge for small group work on its own. The group of four parts plus one or two directing pupils is probably more desirable and manageable in most classrooms than the very large groups needed if pupils work through the entire abridged scene. Subcontracting the sections in this way also means that if you want pupils to present their interpretation and summarise their decision-making for peers, each group can present something that is evidently different rather than sharing that repeats the same lengthy scene. More practical in terms of lesson time, this organisation is more likely to afford sustained consideration of the lines where concentration might otherwise lapse. Whatever the play or the sections for study, this form of allocation can also support differentiation according to the challenge of each part of the play: does one rely on inference more than another? Might one benefit from treatment by pupils with a wider repertoire of acting skills than some of their peers?

Conclusion: bridging active work with writing

If we recall Ollie's direction for pupils to find and highlight moments of tension and emotion, this gives an opportunity to focus on emotion more precisely. In this context pupils can identify the textual details that suggest emotion, and explain how it can be conveyed informed by their performance-based work. If the teacher refers back to the bullet points that started this section (and any others of the teacher's devising) pupils can classify the aspects of performance and introduce the same terminology to their writing. The teacher can help them by showing that sometimes reference to more than one line will make discussion of emotion easier, and examples like this moment in *Henry V* suggest a formula based on juxtaposing one line of stimulus with one for the reaction. The play and scene for study will define the range of adjectives pupils need to describe feelings and the adverbs necessary to capture varying movements. Whether the teacher opts to generate these through spontaneous discussion or more directed activity the principle of generating relevant vocabulary is applicable to all as a crucial means to nuance pupils' writing, and to foster ever more incisive analytic writing that articulates the quality of understanding they derive from engagement in active methods.

References

Andrews, Richard (2008) *Getting Going: Generating, Shaping and Developing Ideas in Writing*. London: Department for Children, Schools and Families.

Boal, Augusto (2008) *Theatre of the Oppressed*. London: Pluto Press.

Bruner, Jerome S. (1966) *Toward a Theory of Instruction*. Cambridge, MA: Belknap Press of Harvard University.

DfE (2013) *English Programmes of Study: Key Stage 3 (National Curriculum in England)*. Reference: DFE-00184-2013.

Fones, Deborah (1999) 'Blocking them in to free them to act', *English in Education*, 35 (3): 21–31.

Gibson, Rex (1998) *Teaching Shakespeare*. Cambridge: Cambridge University Press.

Lewis, Maureen and Wray, David (1996) *Writing Frames: Scaffolding Children's Non-fiction Writing in a Range of Genres*. Reading: University of Reading.

Mercer, Neil (2000) *Words and Minds: How We Use Language to Think Together*. London: Routledge.

Sage, Rosemary (2000) *Class Talk: Successful Learning Through Effective Communication*. Stafford: Network Educational Press.

CHAPTER 10

TEACHING DRAMA IN ENGLISH

Objectives of this chapter:

- To explain the position of drama in the current curriculum
- To explore ways of working with play scripts with classes to emphasise their interpretation in performance and by audiences
- To examine the challenge of bringing scripts alive in class, and how the quality of pupils' response is closely linked with this presentation
- To identify means to help pupils articulate features of plays and their effects through examination of humour in drama

---

Introduction: drama in the English curriculum

This chapter is about drama in the English curriculum. Disappointingly, the conception of drama in that context is narrow. The revised curriculum at Key Stage 4 (DfE, 2014) focuses on plays as an object of literary study, though the extent of pupils' experience will be limited if it matches but does not exceed the requirements to study 'British fiction, poetry or drama since the First World War' and 'two plays by Shakespeare'. The phrase which goes furthest to suggest the unique nature of drama is found in a more general section about 'reading critically'. When applied to plays, this entails 'analysing the ways that great dramatists make their works effective on stage'. This signals drama's affordance as something distinctive, an art form that makes meaning through physical presence, sound, movement and dialogue in a performance space. There are no further references to drama or plays in the Key Stage 4 details, though drama could be linked to the Spoken Language item that describes 'making presentations to argue, inform and entertain, using language for emotional appeal and impact'. The presentational genres mentioned overtly are formal debates and speeches, though effective drama might equally fulfil each of the purposes addressed by these. The Key Stage 3 details parallel these points (DfE, 2013: 50–1), though they anticipate less depth of understanding by pupils. By contrast, Key Stage 2 details make reference to 'role-play and other drama techniques'. They are cited for their capacity to 'help pupils to identify with and explore characters' and their merit in extending pupils' 'understanding of what they read'. Pupils in this phase should also have 'opportunities to try out the language they have listened to' (DfE, 2013: 27). Drama activity is also promoted at this level in support of writing:

> Drama and role-play can contribute to the quality of pupils' writing by providing opportunities for pupils to develop and order their ideas by playing roles and improvising scenes in various settings. (DfE, 2013: 29)

In the requirements for spoken language activity, drama is added to the forms of debate and speech that are sustained across Key Stage 3 and into Key Stage 4 (DfE, 2013: 33). It is curious to see drama integrated into the early key stages but diminished in the latter. In all cases but the last, however, drama activity is presented as a means or stimulus for something else. It is either a prelude to writing or a vehicle for reading and only once (DfE, 2013: 33) is presented without qualification as something inherently valuable. Only here is it mentioned without a brief rationale that prioritises other activities as a reference point.

Returning to reading, pupils in classes across Years 1 and 2 should also be 'listening to and discussing a wide range of fiction, poetry, plays, non-fiction and reference books or textbooks' (DfE, 2013: 40). That sounds like quite passive engagement with plays, and so it is a little surprising to find that from Year 3 (see DfE, 2013: 34) up to Year 6 pupils will be working towards:

preparing poems and plays to read aloud and to perform, showing understanding through intonation, tone and volume so that the meaning is clear to an audience. (2013: 43)

The statement here that pupils will actually *perform* drama seems to signal their only statutory opportunity to do so in terms of the curriculum framework. Beyond that, anything pupils do linked to drama is an enhancement, a step beyond teachers' obligations to the official framework and a result of their choice and judgement. It may also depend on their repertoire. How confident are teachers of English in treating drama as performance rather than literary artefact?

Marcie's lesson plan

Marcie is guiding her Year 10 class in a study of *Educating Rita* by Willy Russell (1985). The play is a 'two-hander', entirely comprised of exchanges between the protagonists Rita and Frank. Rita is a mature student joining a university course for the first time and is intimidated by the prospect. Frank is her tutor in English, though his conversations with her often stray as he shares his own worries and problems with her. The play explores the differences between the two, especially around status and class, and considers the impact the course in higher education has on Rita, and to some extent her husband too (though he is never present as a character, only through reference in the dialogue). While she sets out to 'better herself', the play suggests that whatever changes she goes through are complex and cannot be defined simply as improvement. She may lose something along the way too and find facets of her identity challenged. Through his friendship with Rita, Frank is forced to reflect on his own values too, and he begins to wonder about what exactly his teaching – and its focus, literature – can really achieve.

The lesson is a good one to share, because it concerns teaching drama consistent with the terminology of the new curriculum. It has a focus on the play as a literary object to be analysed and discussed, though it also includes some space for pupils to engage in performance. As such, it is a fair representation of the scope of drama education in the 2014 curriculum: it goes as far as it can with drama while maintaining its focus on literature within the traditional print-oriented emphases of the recent prescription.

Marcie declared the main aim for her lesson in these terms – 'for each pupil to read a part in the play, adopting the appropriate tone and expression'. Through the process of reading the script, she wants her pupils to

become familiar with events and to understand the motivation and intentions of characters. She feels that these aspects are closely connected to
expressive reading: good reading on their part will convey this understanding, through the voice they adopt and whether they can use the appropriate tone. She expects the class to read scene 3 in its entirety within the
lesson. Rita meets Frank to discuss her first essay on E. M. Forster and he
attempts to guide her on what constitutes literature.

Marcie's plan was completed very late in her course of teacher education so she writes only brief activity descriptions because she is very
confident in articulating instructions and guidance spontaneously during
lessons. It is not necessary for her to rehearse them word for word here.
The plan has four phases:

1. Introduction: explain objectives and signal attention to 'tone of voice'
   as a focus. Brief exercise asking pupils to say 'Give me the pencil' in
   three different tones.
2. Class read scene 3. Pupils take on the roles in turn. I allocate, selecting new pupils for each role every 5 minutes. Reminders to adopt
   correct tone as they read. Roles in this scene: Rita, Frank, plus voice
   to read stage directions. Twenty minutes total.
3. Arrange pupils in groups of three to match the roles above. Pupils
   continue reading the next scene. Again, remind pupils to adopt suit-
   able tone of voice. Fifteen minutes total.
4. Plenary phase: each group must report on the scene they have read
   together and share/explain a key event there. Guide class in making
   notes/annotations according to points raised.

The lesson in practice

By this stage in her second placement, Marcie has a very good relationship with her class. It is clear that they have enjoyed the play so far and
that they are interested in both its characters and in its explorations of
class and education.

Marcie successfully organises the whole-class reading phase and the
group work that follows so that she is in control and the lesson has a
purposeful momentum. She teaches the phases she has on her plan and
there is quite fluent development from one part of the lesson to the next.
The pupils enjoy the 'Give me the pencil' exercise, practising the three
tones of voice suggested by Marcie: off-hand, encouraging and irate. As
they try the tones, some find it amusing and a few become self-conscious

with the second and third tones, but on the whole everyone engages well and has success in adopting at least two different tones.

When some pupils take on roles to read in front of the whole class, they begin reading with varied tone for the first two or three lines. Early phrases give them fairly overt cues, such as Rita's opening 'God, I've had enough of this' and Frank's reaction to her paper 'Is it a joke? Is it?', though their attention to tone waivers the further they get into the reading. For one pupil the tones adopted are exaggerated and hit the wrong note. When Marcie attempts to help them through questioning ('What do you think Frank really feels there?') they either respond with a thoughtful answer that has no subsequent effect in their reading or they are unable to interpret correctly. Nevertheless, the way pupils read is otherwise fluent, though much of the scene's humour is missed – or at least it meets with no clear, public acknowledgement through laughter. When Marcie questions the class to elicit their comments on events, they respond well, and they also show continued engagement with the themes of the play. They make apposite remarks about Rita's background and its effect on her confidence (or lack of) in these circumstances. It is clear that there is no general issue with pupils' enjoyment or interest in the play, just that they have found the work around tone challenging.

Similar patterns are apparent in the group reading phase, though in this setting a couple of groups are noticeably voluble as they interrupt one another from time to time to suggest and demonstrate the tone of voice they think might be most appropriate for some lines. Sometimes this leads to a contribution from each member of the group, so that the group hear at least three possible ways of reading the lines in question. The other groups are quieter, and seem more intent on making progress in getting through the scene, not really engaging in experimentation with tone in any audible way.

The plenary is orderly, with each group sharing a comment about key moments pupils identify in the scene. They elaborate, remarking on the feelings of either character or on the themes of the play. Their alertness to those details is clear: they have evidently taken in the sequence of events described in what they have read.

Discussion of the lesson

The lesson was observed by both the class teacher and Marcie's tutor. They concurred in the view that Marcie taught a very well-organised lesson which demonstrated her warm rapport with the pupils. It also demonstrated her secure knowledge of the play and her ability to ask questions likely to develop pupils' thinking about the play. She was always confident in her own comments and was able to respond spontaneously to pupils' remarks and queries.

On speaking with them, Marcie expressed some frustration at not getting as far as she hoped with tone of voice: 'They sort of did it to start with, and then seemed to lose their interest in that as the lesson went on.' Her mentor asked why she thought this might be? Marcie identified tone of voice as a subtle aspect of the play, noting 'I suppose it may not be there on the page for them, so they can't read it if they don't see it.'

In this Marcie has hit on a quality of play scripts that merits a tailored approach, a way of teaching that recognises the distinctive traits of the form. To be realised in performance they need interpretive work. They are intended to be embodied and enacted by performers who lend them a voice and character further to the words. If readers are encountering them on the page, to understand them they must augment the speech attributed to characters with their own ideas and experiences. One difficulty of *Educating Rita* is that it is based on a very particular relationship (between tutor and student) in a setting unfamiliar to pupils. Further, its humour is often subtle, referencing texts and situations that are not only beyond the environment of pupils, but also from another era. Rita can be sardonic and Frank wry, so that pupils need to read between the lines to appreciate some of what they say. If we take those two adjectives 'sardonic' and 'wry' we have two useful terms for describing tone, but neither are words pupils are likely to suggest themselves. If Marcie is to use them, they will need explanation and exemplification for pupils to become comfortable with them. This analysis suggests two dimensions that could benefit from more exact and sustained treatment. The first is focused on tone and giving pupils the verbal resources first to describe a variety of tones with precision and then the capacity to distinguish between various tones within the text. The second strand is the humour, the matter of how to mark out interesting moments for pupils to help them experience and note their humorous effect. This might provide scope for performance-based work, taking pupils away from the desk-based approach of today's lesson and teaching the play as drama as much as treating it as literature.

Teaching about tone

Isolating lines, attributing tone

One technique Marcie can use to help her pupils think carefully about tone is to isolate lines where the tone of voice can significantly affect an audience's interpretation of a line and their response. If she adapts the pattern of three she tried with her 'Give me the pencil' exercise, she can present the pupils with three lines drawn from the play which she knows require distinct tones. Two sets of lines she might use, sharing the same first item, are:

A
Frank: Is it a joke? Is it?
Rita: I thought reading was supposed to be good for one.
Rita: I'm dead ignorant y'know.

and

B
Frank: Is it a joke? Is it?
Frank: It'll be your hard luck when he [the examiner] fails your paper.
Frank: Devouring pulp fiction is not being well read.

Marcie can exploit these juxtaposed lines in several ways. With set A, she might ask pupils to suggest what tone might be apt for each. Here the fact of the difference between examples is an aid to pupils' awareness that they work differently and for different effects. Alternatively, she might wish to structure things so that pupils are guided to a distinction. For instance, she may select three lines akin to set B that signal Frank's diminishing impatience with Rita as he better understands her circumstances and perspective. Marcie can state that fact to pupils – 'All of these show that Frank is calming down' – and then ask them to place them in order of degree: which one shows Frank at his most angry, which is relatively the most patient, and which goes in-between? Having identified the sequence, can pupils explain how they are different? If there is easy access to thesauri, pupils can look up synonyms for 'irritated' or 'impatient' and work to identify a continuum from most to least irritated, strongly to mildly impatient. Another variation would be to supply pupils with ten adjectives describing tone, three of which match the lines pupils have. Can they select the three adjectives best suited to the lines, and attribute one to each?

These exercises present analysis of tone as an exercise in discernment, but also require deploying (and having) a vocabulary sufficiently precise to express subtle distinctions. In that regard, pupils need to know about a range of emotions that extends beyond 'happy' or 'sad' and have a vocabulary that gives them more than the colloquial 'gutted' to express disappointment. While an activity like this can support vocabulary development, it is less good at supporting pupils' sensitivity to the representation of emotions and inner psychology. For that, dramatic activity brings new possibilities that combine cognitive and affective response.

Using lines for mini-plays – tone and context

One technique Marcie can use to help pupils consider the meaning and tone of lines is to draw them out of the play, isolate them and present them for pupils to work with creatively. This involves them incorporating the ready-made lines in their own improvisations, and building dialogue and gesture around them. The process can be adapted for use in scripts constructed by the pupils too, if the teacher finds this more practical than performance-based work. In this scene, a few well-chosen lines convey a narrative likely to resonate with pupils' knowledge of school and study:

Pupil lines:

God, I've had enough of this. It's borin'.
Don't go on at me.
I'm dead ignorant.

Teacher lines:

Is it a joke? Is it?
Don't mention it in an exam.

This activity can work in pairs or in groups because everyone can contribute to suggesting a sequence using the lines and to what the characters could say around them even if they can't participate as performers. To construct their own scenes, pupils must give the lines a context, and must therefore imagine a situation and interaction between people. As a consequence, they may deploy the lines in contrast to Russell. When it comes to sharing these scenes with the class, groups will use the lines in varying situations and with differing interpretations. These can shed light on the lines when encountered in the context of the original scene. Because pupils have experienced these as triggers for interpretive work, they are ready to see the possibilities they suggest and can at least read the play with confidence, with attention now on what these mean in the new context instead of basic comprehension. It is a technique that can be adapted for the study of any play. A limited version of this activity works with single lines. Inevitably this emphasises the chosen item and has the potential to support pupils in memorising key quotations. An extended version, giving pupils enough lines to shape a whole new scene, perhaps has less creative scope but directs their attention to the connections *between* lines. In building the full dialogue they have to decide what is omitted and what could pass in the gaps, in doing so speculating about the nature of the relationship and the motivation of each character.

Improvising parallel conversations – tone and feeling

Marcie could opt to defer attention to the play for some time, instead prefiguring it in activity designed to help pupils explore the nature of Frank and Rita's relationship and the emotions that influence their exchange. For Marcie, this entails identifying a key exchange in the play and transforming it into a set of instructions for pupils. This should anonymise characters and describe the interaction in straightforward neutral terms, probably in the form of bullet points. As such it sets out the guidelines for the pupils as actors but does not present them with a script. It provides the prompts for improvisation but parallels an exchange in the play in a format like this:

> Person A complains that he/she is fed up with the reading they must do for their course.
>
> Person B tells Person A that Person A's essay is not of the required standard.
>
> Person A is defensive.

… and so on. If Marcie shapes this with care, it can give pupils the stimulus to explore in improvisation the attitudes and behaviour in a similar situation. They can use their own words, their own movements, and can suggest what people in those circumstances might think or feel.

Marcie can give her pupils time to improvise an exchange according to the guidance, then allow pairs to share their work. If she wants, she can ask questions to encourage elaboration, perhaps asking the pupils-in-role to comment further on why they make particular remarks or to explain what's in their mind as they utter something. Is what they say the same as what they mean?

Once pupils have performed exchanges for each other the class can move to the text. Marcie can introduce the reading with a cue signalling the parallel between pupils' role play and the corresponding exchange in the script. The first exercise prefigured what they encounter here in the play, and aims to support their understanding where otherwise they could miss subtle aspects of tone. Marcie can draw on what pupils have already shared, for example by saying 'So when Rita says this, remember how Hannah [or any other pupil] spoke in her exchange. Rita uses the same agitated tone here', or by suggesting a connection in characters' motives: 'Barney explained why his character acted in that way. Do you think Frank has similar motives?'

Humour: making texts laughable

Humour in the curriculum

Quite frequently, teachers of English guide their classes in the study of texts that are humorous. Amusing texts are very common at A-level, whether the overtly comedic plays of Tom Stoppard, in the rich narratorial asides of Dickens, J. G. Farrell (see *The Siege of Krishnapur*) or Winterson (*Oranges Are Not the Only Fruit*), or in satirical works such as *Slaughterhouse 5* and *Gulliver's Travels*. Wilde's *The Importance of Being Earnest* has had a place on both GCSE and A-level specifications, while most of his other plays have appeared as options for advanced study. In Key Stages 3 and 4, humour can be found in commonly taught novels (the dry wit of Louis Sachar's *Holes* is a good example) but most often in plays. Sometimes this is problematic, as pupils' introduction to the forms of comedy and tragedy as categories – usually with regard to Shakespeare – may coincide with their analysis of comic scenes in tragedies such as *Romeo and Juliet*. In that play the scene in which the Nurse banters with Mercutio and Romeo (Act 2, scene 4) is often considered in terms of comic relief to the building tension in antagonism between the Montague and Capulet families. Pupils may have to modify their understanding of comedy as a form at the same time as they are asked to analyse texts according to their humorous impact. Here they are required to explain how the audience is made to laugh, so they must understand and articulate how the play constructs humour. That is not an easy thing to do, which may explain why the number of humorous texts available for study increases only at A-level.

A few years ago, the government department with responsibility for teacher education circulated video training material showing an English student teacher guiding her Year 9 class in the study of *Romeo and Juliet* (TTA, 2001). The lesson presented showed her helping the class to respond to an examination question about 'the Nurse scene'. The question made the demands described above, asking pupils 'How does the Nurse add humour to the play?' The footage of the lesson and the supplementary booklet including the teacher's lesson plans made clear her good work in helping pupils identify humorous lines and the time she gave for them to explain why individual lines were amusing. All of this was useful and extended their engagement with the humour, though at no point in the footage of the lesson do we hear pupils actually laugh at the play. Many teachers will recognise this situation, that the comic dimension of a play can be lost in classroom study. Potentially hilarious lines or events can be passed over without any obvious reaction from the class, as if they are just part of a flow of text that receives unvarying and neutral response. If teachers have taught the same plays to a few classes, they may also find varying reactions. Some groups do find details funny and dwell on them, yet when the same teacher uses a similar approach elsewhere, other classes remain impassive or unimpressed, if not bewildered. Evidently the humorous aspects of texts can be challenging for the teacher to realise in the classroom.

Comedy, categories and the classroom

We should take that verb 'realise' seriously. A better response, and deeper understanding to support analysis, is more likely if we can make the humour inherent in texts come alive for the pupils. The first step is to experience humour in the classroom, ideally to provoke laughter, through examples of comedy in performance. This doesn't have to mean performing the study text in the sense of acting it out to 'get' the humour. That would need skill and confidence in performance and is not a straightforward process without very talented and confident pupils participating. Introducing humour in performance can exploit radio, television and film resources first to give pupils the chance to encounter humour through examples enjoyed communally, and second as a means to illustrate and then describe *types* of humour. If pupils can recognise that humour can be created through various means, they are likely to offer more focused and precise responses to texts. They will be better equipped to *analyse* humour, to do more than observe where humour occurs (whether they laughed or not).

Radio is mentioned in the list above very deliberately, because sharing examples of radio comedy inevitably draws attention to how you can be funny through words and sounds. Programmes that use word-play, silly voices and repetition, and which provide examples of a well-executed punchline, can give pupils clear instances of verbal humour. If these are carefully selected by the teacher as instances likely to amuse pupils then all the better. They can enjoy them first. If they laugh, the teacher has an easy way in: 'What was funny about that?', and further, 'How were words used to make us laugh?' Depending on the phase of teaching, the teacher may also draw on established academic considerations of the comic, such as Henri Bergson's *Laughter* (1911). Its second chapter explores 'the comic element in words', attending to wit, metaphor, punning, irony, exaggeration and parody. It also includes very interesting passages on the comic potential of jargon, and on the humour inherent in using 'terms of utmost respectability' to describe 'some scandalous situation, some low-class calling or disgraceful behaviour'. This latter practice especially, Bergson asserts, is characteristically English!

The contrast with visual humour can be marked with use of silent film excerpts (Chaplin would be the obvious choice, or maybe Harold Lloyd or Buster Keaton) or modern sequences of wordless slapstick and physical humour (for instance in the work of Vic Reeves and Bob Mortimer). In viewing these, and hopefully after genuine amusement for some, pupils can begin to describe the sort of movements, expressions and incidents that provoke humour. One dimension of the visual examples that may parallel the affordance of those in sound is the way humour can depend on the presentation of events in time: how do things build up, leading to a surprise juxtaposition of words, a sentence that undercuts everything that went before, or a sudden action or fall?

Seeing instances of humour in performance is essential if pupils are to link describing how it is created with its effect on audience members. Where pupils enjoy modern texts, and especially if they are genuinely amused, the teacher can create an atmosphere where they may be more ready to notice the humour in a play script. In addition to having access to examples maintaining spoken comedy and visual comedy as discrete categories, it helps if pupils can see examples where the spoken and visual combine. This could give an opportunity to recognise comedy arising from specific situations (predictably, some attention to situation comedy may be useful), to comedy of exaggeration or parody, to political satire and to genre pastiche (such as *Monty Python's Holy Grail*, *The Day Today*). In work with *Romeo and Juliet* around this question of the Nurse, it would be necessary to select texts that anticipate the forms of humour apparent in the scene and use them to introduce pupils to the relevant descriptive vocabulary. It is even better if you can find a modern example that mirrors multiple features of the scene for comparable effect.

You can apply the same approach to the scene under discussion in Marcie's lesson, though you might take special note of the 'two-handedness' of Russell's play. This is not a play of energetic slapstick action, but it is a play of a 'fish out of water', a common trope in comedy drama. Any comedy example in which characters of contrasting social background meet could emphasise the differing cultural reference points and registers of speech of Rita and Frank in this script. While these broad classifications are useful, there needs to be some further work to help pupils explain the mechanics of their exchange. Explaining how comedy derives from these differences is challenging, and the potential sources of humour may need to be itemised quite deliberately by the teacher.

Comedy can derive from misunderstandings, especially where characters believe they are speaking about the same thing but where they have very different outlooks. Bergson describes such circumstances as 'equivocal situations', where the audience know its 'real meaning' though the understanding of characters is only partial. If such misunderstandings are to be found funny by the audience, this entails their own ability to recognise the difference between the two, and perhaps to be gently unsettled by the discomfort of one character or another. Sometimes they may align with one character rather than another. In *Educating Rita* we have to know something of distinctions between high and low culture, especially around literature, to appreciate that Rita is adrift in terms of the references Frank makes in conversation. If we understand that, we must also have privileged cultural knowledge that puts us closer to Frank in this situation than to Rita. This corresponds with a superiority theory of humour, consistent with Hobbes' explanation 'that the passion of laughter is nothing else but sudden glory arising from some sudden conception of some eminency in ourselves, by comparison with the infirmity of others, or with our own formerly' (Hobbes, 1889). This may also account for humour derived from notions of appropriate conduct in given situations and deviations from those expectations. Rita is not familiar with the ground rules of a university tutorial, asking questions that are more direct than Frank expects, commenting without reverence on the reputations of authors, and not recognising the etiquette of tutorial behaviour even in her movement around his office.

Conclusion

Whatever the text for classroom study, time will be limited for the essential activities of reading the text, developing pupils' responses and helping them articulate those orally and in writing. Scope for in-depth study of humour will be limited, and in any case will be shaped by the characteristics of the text in hand. If Marcie were to address humour in *Educating Rita*, she might take the following steps:

1. *To create a classroom receptive to humour.* Pre-empt analysis of humour in the play by sharing with pupils recorded performances (audio or video) with similar features. These might include examples

of other comic texts that parallel the situation in the play for study, for example of two characters from different social backgrounds and different status. They may also include instances of dry wit, sarcasm, malapropism and punning.

2. *To describe the context for humour in the study text.* Use the resources to build pupils' capacity to explain how humour derives from social awkwardness. Pupils will need deliberate introduction to terms such as class, status, social awkwardness and 'fish out of water'. If analysis influenced by superiority theory is introduced, it may be preferable to introduce it with these texts, with the emphasis less on defining the theory and more on helping pupils structure sentences that describe how the audience, in finding the humour in a situation, must find alignment with a 'superior' and more knowing perspective.

3. *To identify and label types of humour.* Following a similar method, introduce terminology that pinpoints types of humour (as indicated in point 1 above), ensuring they have the vocabulary to describe the types the teacher has identified, but also allowing space for pupils to contribute their own vocabulary or expressions.

4. *To cue shared reading of the study text.* Introduce and read the relevant scene, possibly providing cues for pupils before reading to signal the connections with preparatory work: for example 'Like the extract we watched from *The Wrong Mans*, this is an exchange between two people. This is also a 'fish-out-of-water' comedy …', or 'See if you can make any connections between what we read now and *The Class Sketch* (the BBC sketch with Ronnie Barker, Ronnie Corbett and John Cleese) we saw earlier …' With *Educating Rita* there is always the option to use the film too, which might help pupils see similarities more easily.

5. *To apply understanding of humour to details in the text.* To shape activity in which pupils begin to identify lines or exchanges that create humour. This could involve attributing terms like 'dry wit' and 'malapropism' to lines through annotation, though it can be transformed into a more creative activity if pupils work in groups, enlisted in the capacity of directors. If they are instructed to advise actors to 'convey your dry wit here' or 'use a sarcastic tone here' they can select the lines that they believe need such emphasis and guide one another in expression of the lines, possibly in a forum-theatre approach like the one described earlier in this chapter. This sort of work also allows space to explore the director's decisions, and in particular to answer the question 'how will that amuse the audience?'

These steps equip pupils with some verbal resources to go beyond merely identifying instances of humour, to improve the precision of their descriptions and helping them explain how humour is constructed. With some vocabulary at their disposal and activities which help them verbalise how humour works on – or, better, *with* – the audience, they can write about humour with greater success.

This chapter has focused on humour as a core trait of many drama texts, but also as an area that can be challenging to teach. The five steps outlined in this concluding section can also be applied to other features, such as dramatic tension and irony, to delineating tragedy, or to specific conventions such as soliloquy. Play scripts remain central to English, so it is inevitable that you will need to engage with some of these features in your early work as a teacher of English. Where the current secondary curriculum emphasises treatment of drama as literature, this approach bridges the treatment of drama as performance with written analysis. Crucially, it *requires* attention to performance as a foundation for engagement and intelligent scrutiny.

References

Bergson, H. (1911) *Laughter*. Temple of Earth Publishing. Online at: http://www.templeofearth.com. (accessed 1 October 2014)

DfE (2013) *English Programmes of Study: Key Stage 3 (National Curriculum in England)*. Reference: DFE-00184-2013.

DfE (2014) *English Programmes of Study: Key Stage 4 (National Curriculum in England)*. Reference: DFE-00497-2014.

Farrell, J. G. (1996) *Siege of Krishnapur*. London: Phoenix.

Hobbes, Thomas (1889) 'Laughter', item 13, part 1, chapter 9, pp. 41–2, in F. Tönnies (ed.) (1969) *The Elements of Law: Natural and Politic by Thomas Hobbes*, 2nd edn. London: Frank Cass.

Russell, Willy (1981/1989) *Educating Rita*. London: Longman.

Sachar, Louis (2000) *Holes*. London: Bloomsbury.

Shakespeare, William (1595/2005) *Romeo and Juliet*. Cambridge: Cambridge Schools Shakespeare.

Swift, Jonathan (1726/2003) *Gulliver's Travels*. London: Penguin Classics.

Teacher Training Agency (2001) *Supporting Assessment for the Award of Qualified Teacher Status* (video). London: Teacher Training Agency.

Vonnegut, Kurt (1970/2000) *Slaughterhouse 5*. London: Vintage.

Winterson, Jeanette (1985) *Oranges Are Not the Only Fruit*. London: Vintage.

Wilde, Oscar (1899/2001) *The Importance of Being Earnest*. London: Penguin Classics.

CHAPTER 11

TEACHING POETRY

Objectives of this chapter:

- To examine teaching focused on imagery in poetry
- To consider lesson design and how to conceptualise a lesson so that it has coherence reflecting both the poem and the skill or response you want pupils to develop
- To explore the significance of the teacher's understanding of the poem as the basis for shaping challenging and appropriately supportive lessons for pupils

Introduction

In this chapter Martine's lesson sets out to develop pupils' understanding of imagery in Wilfred Owen's *Dulce Et Decorum Est* (see Hudson, 1988, or any similar anthology).

The poem is widely taught at GCSE and A-level, usually in anthologies gathered around the theme of war. Sometimes these focus solely on the 1914–18 conflict but they can be broader in scope. The immediate discussion will make some reference to other poetry on the same theme, but concentrates on imagery as the generic issue relevant to the study of poetry across all levels whatever the unifying theme of the collection. In particular, how can you help pupils respond to imagery with attention to subtle detail? Often this entails recognising that imagery can work on readers or listeners to varying effect, so the task of the teacher can involve classifying the imagery to support pupils in articulating the distinctive work of any single example. This also makes it easier for pupils to contrast the effects of images across poems. The more precise they can be about how one image operates, the more likely it will be that they can understand how another shapes our thoughts or feelings in a different way.

The notion of levels of reading (Guppy and Hughes, 1999) is relevant here, recognising that when pupils consider imagery they usually have to read in several ways at once (for instance, see Fenton (2002), Hughes (1967) and Padel (2002) for accounts of its varied impact). Imagery can be direct, almost photographic in character, using carefully selected vocabulary to identify objects and details. This type is demonstrated in the line 'Candles and braziers glinted through the chinks / And curtain-flaps of dug-outs' from Siegfried Sassoon's poem *A Working Party* (again, see Hudson, 1988, or similar). It conveys pictures to the reader mainly through concrete nouns. Its relationship with the world is one of labelling, in such a way that we know exactly the objects that populate the scene and can thus visualise them. We find no adjectives or adverbs here. The verb 'glinted' is the only word that can signal to us any sort of perspective, less neutral than an alternative like 'were seen'.

Other forms of imagery may be crafted to make us think differently, figurative language affording readers greater scope to bring their own associations to the text. From the same poem, the concluding lines show this other work:

> ... then a flare
> Gave one white glimpse of No Man's Land and wire;
> And as he dropped his head the instant split
> His startled life with lead, and all went out.

The reader has to do more than see the labelled items (head, wire). Even the noun phrase No Man's Land requires that we read 'beyond the lines', as it assumes our knowledge of the term and its significance. In 'one white glimpse' words draw on our understanding of the action of a flare but also combine to enact it, signalling its unique split-second life in both 'one' and 'glimpse'. It is possible the phrase recalls for the reader flash photography, even images of flare-lit trenches from film and television (for example, in the BBC's *Parade's End*). This imagery makes meaning 'between the lines' too, using visible and concrete detail to convey the moment of the soldier's death when the intangible force of life is extinguished. The lines give us the direct, mundane 'he dropped his head', the hard substance of lead, the physical action of splitting, yet it is an incorporeal and ephemeral moment, this specific 'instant', that is the subject responsible for the action of splitting, sundering equally insubstantial vitality. The use of an adjective in 'startled life' gives existence an expression, a face, and we know that when 'all went out' this does more than create a mental image of darkness. It accrues transcendental and symbolic status.

Martine's lesson

Martine has worked with a Year 9 class for some time, teaching a scheme of work designed by her placement department and focused on poetry of the First World War. She hasn't been able to select the poems used, as they are provided by the department in a prepared anthology for pupils. Today she is leading a lesson focused on Owen's *Dulce Et Decorum Est* and uses both an audio version and the printed version:

> Bent double, like old beggars under sacks,
> Knock-kneed, coughing like hags, we cursed through sludge,
> Till on the haunting flares we turned our backs
> And towards our distant rest began to trudge.
> Men marched asleep. Many had lost their boots
> But limped on, blood-shod. All went lame; all blind;
> Drunk with fatigue; deaf even to the hoots
> Of disappointed shells that dropped behind.
>
> GAS! Gas! Quick, boys! – An ecstasy of fumbling,
> Fitting the clumsy helmets just in time;
> But someone still was yelling out and stumbling
> And floundering like a man in fire or lime …
> Dim, through the misty panes and thick green light
> As under a green sea, I saw him drowning.
>
> In all my dreams, before my helpless sight,
> He plunges at me, guttering, choking, drowning.

If in some smothering dreams you too could pace
Behind the wagon that we flung him in,
And watch the white eyes writhing in his face,
His hanging face, like a devil's sick of sin;
If you could hear, at every jolt, the blood
Come gargling from the froth-corrupted lungs,
Obscene as cancer, bitter as the cud
Of vile, incurable sores on innocent tongues, –
My friend, you would not tell with such high zest
To children ardent for some desperate glory,
The old Lie: Dulce et decorum est
Pro patria mori.

She starts the lesson by sharing objectives with pupils, and shows them a PowerPoint slide:

Learning objectives

- To develop your understanding of the imagery the poet uses to portray the experience of warfare.
- To comment on how the poet creates a vivid picture of the trenches.
- To write a paragraph commenting on how the imagery creates a picture for you.

She reads these aloud and gives some further verbal explanation of the term imagery, asking pupils to think about the concept like a 'film in the head': how words help you see scenes, people and details in your mind, changing as the poem develops.

Martine plays pupils the audio version of the poem twice and they have the printed version on their desks in front of them on each occasion.

The rest of the lesson has four stages, the first three tied directly to the objectives.

The first phase considers stanza 1, with Martine commenting on the opening two lines. She asks pupils to imagine the posture of the soldiers and points out the use of simile in each line. She invites pupils to make a verbal comment about the imagery in the stanza that they found put a picture in their mind and encourages them to elaborate on how this relates to examples seen in poems studied earlier in the scheme.

In the next phase she guides activity to address the second objective, initially exploring the meaning of 'vivid', paraphrasing with words such as 'powerful', 'strong' and 'clear'. She asks pupils to identify details that they personally find vivid in the second stanza and the isolated couplet that follows, and to tell their neighbour about the picture it creates for them.

In the third phase, she guides plenary comment about the final stanza. Four pupils offer comment on vivid imagery here. Martine uses pupils' comments to annotate the slide of the stanza that she concurrently displays for pupils on the interactive whiteboard. Martine then asks all pupils to select at least one example of imagery in this stanza and to write a paragraph explaining how it creates a picture for them.

In the last phase of the lesson, Martine asks some pupils to read their paragraphs aloud. To conclude, other pupils are asked to identify good examples in their peers' writing where they explained how Owen created vivid imagery.

Comment on Martine's lesson

Martine's lesson has much to commend it. It is possible to see the lesson's coherence in the relationship between each phase of activity and the stated objectives. It remains focused on the matter of imagery throughout. It also suggests her commitment to eliciting and fostering pupils' response in the various opportunities for them to comment on the poem. It recognises too that pupils might respond differently to the poem depending on its mode of presentation: she offers it on the page and in sound. Finally, it accommodates writing, preparing pupils through discussion as means to rehearse the analytic comment they must commit to paper. Martine's lesson shows she is aware that writing needs guided support and that though talk around the poem is important and necessary, on its own it does not suffice as preparation for the examination-based assessment that concludes this study. Any evaluation of Martine's lesson needs to recognise these strengths, comprising as they do a solid foundation for teaching. At the same time, taking a view that observation and feedback is concerned with developing her practice for the future, we need to consider how we help Martine widen her repertoire. What else can she do to teach in this way even more effectively, with even more impact?

There is scope for Martine to plan the lesson so that she guides pupils not only in understanding and commenting on imagery in this poem, but also such that they refine their understanding of imagery itself. By considering the different ways images in this poem work, Martine could teach her pupils *ways* of discussing imagery as well as how to discuss imagery per se.

As with *A Working Party*, successive uses of imagery create pictures in varying ways. They orient readers to the phenomena and experiences distinctively too: one instance works differently from the next. That is evident enough in the first two lines. It is reasonable and conventional enough for Martine to draw attention to the use of simile, and by this stage her pupils are very familiar with the idea that a simile compares one thing or idea with another, usually to accentuate a shared quality. What identifying similes can't do, however, is to explain the cumulative effect of imagery in these opening phrases. 'Bent double' is transparent, but when followed by 'like old beggars under sacks', the compound adjective 'knock-kneed' and a second simile referencing 'hags', there is an intensification of our sense of the uncomfortable stooped gait with which the soldiers move. Each of these separate images has scope to conjure the hunched posture. The literal examples describe physical features, while each simile evokes figures generally represented as having distorted frames. That the beggars of the first are 'under sacks' manipulates a visible, concrete referent to additionally suggest tactile and suffocating or burdensome qualities. The second example doesn't really describe a visible phenomenon. The focus is on the act of 'coughing', though 'hags' specifies the nature of the cough and lends the discomfort physical form. While we wouldn't expect pupils to discuss the lines in quite this detail, this brief analysis shows that their comment could take one of many directions, and it indicates the subtleties they might probe. If we classify these traits, one could be termed cumulative, while a second characteristic of imagery to consider will be the nature of the appeal it makes: which sense(s) does it stimulate, if any, beyond the visual? Does it do more than just work on the mind's eye?

Conceptualising the lesson

One approach Martine might take to refine her teaching is to find a way of conceptualising the poem based on what she finds in it. This does not mean she needs to alter what she already has in the plan. The sequence of the lesson, the sort of understanding it fosters and the skills it develops are each important and need retaining. To conceptualise the poem Martine needs to identify a single idea that concurrently complements the detail of the text, the focus she has chosen of imagery and which can provide an anchor for pupils as they make progress with the text and in their learning. If Martine can find a central idea that does these things she can make the coherence of the lesson more overt for pupils, and underline aspects of the text that could help them comment with more nuance about the text before them.

Close attention to imagery helps us find changing use by Owen stanza by stanza. The changes in use revolve around point of view, a different perspective in each on events in the immediate environment of the trenches. If we look again at Martine's learning objectives for the lesson, we can see how getting at these shifts in use is relevant. The first objective concerned developing 'understanding of the imagery the poet uses to portray the experience of warfare'. If pupils can recognise that imagery is used in differing ways, and can be given precise means to do so, it is possible that more of the class will demonstrate learning consistent with this objective but also showing greater sophistication. We can see the scope for the poem to challenge pupils' skills of analysis. Similar principles apply if we consider the second learning objective, 'to comment on how the poet creates a vivid picture of the trenches'. Martine's lesson gave opportunities for pupils to comment on pictures the poem creates for them, and they had space to explain how the pictures affected them specifically, but there was no part of the lesson that *developed* their understanding of how imagery can work. Without this component, the lesson could not provide pupils with opportunity to *express* the workings of imagery. For Martine, then, the task is to build on the already sound foundation of her lesson with precise thought about how pupils will become better able to distinguish uses of imagery and more skilled in articulating how it is used. While some of what Martine considers necessarily has aspects that cannot be disentwined from this particular poem, the more subtle orientation to imagery that she supports will be applicable to other poems and to texts in other forms.

Dulce Et Decorum Est is structured in three parts, each of eight lines and each in *abab* schemes where rhymes come in alternate lines. Strictly speaking it has four stanzas, as the second section of eight lines is split with a line break, so that it falls in a group of six and then an isolated pair. This means too that the split divorces rhymes from one another where the *abab* pattern is disrupted. That there is this break in the pattern directs our attention to the lines set apart:

> In all my dreams, before my helpless sight,
> He plunges at me, guttering, choking, drowning.

Given Martine's interest in how Owen uses imagery to create a vivid picture of the trenches, these are a powerful starting point as they provide a clear if disturbing description of the dying soldier's last flailing, tortured moments. If she chooses, she could explore why the image is so disturbing. Is it the movement of the dying soldier towards the persona voicing the poem ('plunges at me')? Is it the combination of 'guttering, choking, drowning', intensifying the pain through the list? Is it the figurative use of 'drowning' (in gas, as it follows from the previous lines, 'as under a green sea')? The disturbance could be in our sense that this image haunts the persona 'in all my dreams', that the obscenity of this death can only be conveyed as a nightmare arriving unbidden and overwhelming his 'helpless sight'. All are viable directions for exploration and each indicates something quite different about how the imagery of the two lines works.

Before coming to the analysis of imagery, let us pause to reflect on the ethical dimension (see Meek, 1987). On the one hand, Martine has an aim of developing her pupils' skills of literary analysis around imagery. She also has a broader aim, not articulated in her lesson objectives, of fostering pupils' appreciation of literature over time, and their confidence in approaching it. Studying this poem makes evident that appreciation is something other than enjoyment: if understood, if 'appreciated', the poem disturbs the reader. The ethical consideration for any teacher working with imagery likely to disturb readers is to what extent should they deliberately promote the full force of the imagery, to assist pupils in seeing the unsettling pictures in the mind's eye? If this were a 'film in the head', some of these pictures might be subject to censorship, deemed inappropriate for viewing in school or by under-18s. The same is true of imagery in *Macbeth*, say, or *Titus Andronicus*, or in poetry such as Yeats' 'Leda and the Swan'. If pupils really do 'get' the imagery they co-construct dark visions, though the implications of this for their emotional response is sometimes overlooked in teaching where literary analysis is the ostensible focus. Yet this must be a consideration for the teacher if 'how poets create vivid pictures' is addressed properly. These examples of imagery are intended to disturb, so pupils cannot speak about how they work unless they do formulate mental pictures in response.

The details of *Dulce Et Decorum Est* offer some solution to this pastoral dilemma that is also consistent with the analytical skills to be developed. Where the isolated pair of lines describe 'my helpless sight' they offer an anchor for study of the poem. Martine can make 'sight' the core concept at the heart of her teaching, and by doing so immediately brings into play the matter of perspective. Reference to sight can be found in each stanza of the poem, whether full, inhibited ('helpless') or lost ('blind'). While it may be useful to trace these instances, Martine can challenge pupils to more advanced response by also noting the shifts in perspective. The separated lines we started with clearly belong to the point of view of the persona, a fact corroborated in the preceding sestet's use of the first person in 'I saw him drowning'. That these lines describe what the persona sees in dreams adds to our information around that central idea of sight: the persona himself distinguishes between what he sees in actuality and the pictures in his own mind's eye, though the two are linked and the imagery of dreams becomes more potent. The preceding stanza not only attributes perspective, it also locates it and conveys the nature of perception: 'Dim, through the misty panes and thick green light / As under a green sea'. The simile here signals a mode of perception other than usual, and though this is not a picture of the imagination as in dreams, it has to be described as a distorted, mediated version of reality.

The first stanza does something different with sight. For the most part what is seen is not attributed to a specific perspective. We know about the party of soldiers ('we cursed through sludge') but instead of learning which details draw their attention, we are given details instead about sight denied. In the third line, 'on the haunting flares we turned our backs' shows their choice in looking away from the eerie light, but by the end of the stanza a metaphorical blindness falls on all ('All went lame; all blind'). If we trace development in how Owen uses sight in the poem, it seems that in the stanza of most concrete description sight is unattributed and diminishes until it is lost. In the second, what is seen is precisely attributed but what is witnessed cannot be accepted by the onlooker as real: it is mediated figuratively or in the imagery of dreams. In the third stanza, conversely, the reader or listener is invited to join the scene in dreams themselves, to 'pace/Behind the wagon' carrying the dying man and 'watch the white eyes writhing in his face'.

Martine's lesson can look at imagery but additionally trace how the use of imagery changes over the poem, particularly with regard to the point of view from which these images are perceived. The overt acknowledgement of perspective, encompassing whether images exist in actuality or in dreams, can also act as a distancing device by which to manage the disturbing impact of Owen's imagery.

Conceptualising the poem: putting it into practice

How can Martine tie this approach with the strengths of her original lesson? Remember, that lesson had a good structure and included time for pupils to rehearse ideas about the poem before putting pen to paper. She can keep much the same shape here, but can exploit the structure to guide pupils' writing more closely.

Her first lesson had four phases beyond the opening phase in which pupils first encountered the poem. In the revised lesson, the possible changes to each phase depend on the opening phase also changing so that pupils are aware of the importance of sight in the poem. Martine would be advised to follow sharing the full poem with pupils with some attention to the isolated pair of lines, probably conveying her own interest in the way it creates pictures in our minds. She can also maintain control of discussion around this image, acknowledging that she finds it disturbing and signalling to pupils something of Owen's intent with reference to the poem's political statement, to subvert the 'old Lie' referenced in the title that it is sweet and fitting to die for one's country. Owen set out to present imagery that would counter that position.

Figure 11.1 describes the changes that could follow, which have the common feature of contributing to progress in pupils' writing more directly than Martine's first version.

Original lesson	Possible change
Considers stanza 1. Martine guides close attention to first two lines and use of simile. Pupils make verbal comment about further imagery that creates picture for them, making links with other poems of war studied previously.	Considers stanza 1. Martine first asks pupils to identify and share details that contribute to their mental picture of the soldiers' movement in the trenches. She then asks pupils to consider what we know the soldiers see or don't see. She points out that soldiers become 'blind' – in what way? What is Owen trying to convey? Martine shares with the class a paragraph she has drafted herself. It explains how Owen gives details that contribute to our mental images of the soldiers. It contrasts this with the fact that the soldiers themselves become 'blind'.
Focus on vivid imagery, with pupils selecting examples from the second stanza and the two lines that follow. Pupils share comment about the selected image with their neighbour.	Because Martine's example in phase one embeds quotations and builds comment around them it provides a model for their writing. It also introduces discussion of sight to the piece. In this phase Martine poses questions for students about the perspective on events. Who is seeing the events? How do we know? Where are they? How do they feel about the events? Which events are real and which not (i.e. are dreamt)? She gives pupils between 5 and 10 minutes to explore these with a neighbour and elicits responses to each question in plenary discussion. She introduces a second paragraph of writing that builds on her first: *In this stanza and the two lines that follow, Owen gives us a different perspective. We are still in among the soldiers, but this time we see things from the point of view of one soldier. Owen tells us that he sees …* *Owen's technique of giving readers information through the eyes of one soldier …*

(Continued)

Figure 11.1 (Continued)

	The paragraph is only partially complete, but Martine provides sentence stems that encourage pupils to address the impact of perspective on our response to Owen's imagery.
	Martine gives pupils time to write in order to extend and complete the paragraph, encouraging them to draw on responses to the questions asked at the start.
	The phase concludes with Martine asking a couple of pupils to share what they have written. Having monitored their writing, Martine selects examples that demonstrate fluent and embedded use of quotation, and which are successful in conveying the impact of the imagery cited.
Whole-class discussion of the final stanza. The teacher annotates a copy of the stanza via the interactive whiteboard. Pupils select one example of imagery in the stanza and then complete their own paragraph explaining how it creates a picture for them.	In this phase Martine guides pupils to greater independence in their written response to the poem, while also developing their awareness of the shifting perspective across stanzas. She asks pupils to note Owen's invitation to 'you' the reader to follow the wagon and watch. Why do you think Owen makes this invitation? Can you explain the invitation any better by looking at the poem's last four lines?
	She gives pupils time in pairs to reflect on these, and then asks pupils to continue their writing. She gives them some supporting prompts.
	Your paragraph will comment on:
	• *the change in point of view from stanzas two and three* • *how the new point of view makes you respond to the imagery* • *one or two images that are most powerful for you in contradicting the 'old Lie' that it is sweet and fitting to die at war for your country.*
	Martine gives pupils at least ten minutes to continue their writing.

Figure 11.1   Possible changes to Martine's poetry lesson

As in the original lesson, Martine should include a plenary phase where pupils can share examples of their writing. Here though she can if she chooses ask pupils to engage in some self- or peer-assessment, as this new structure gives scope for pupils to contrast the paragraph written with more autonomy with one of the earlier, more directed paragraphs (see Marshall (2004) and Marshall and Wiliam (1990) for commentaries concerning these forms of assessment in English). How well does it express the different way imagery is used? Does it make clear how our response is also influenced by point of view? If she chooses not to direct pupils to these considerations, she can remark on shared examples that exhibit success along these lines. In addition, pupils have completed not just one paragraph but instead have a sequence of three that show development and coherence around the exploration of a common idea. It is a better, more sophisticated blueprint for the writing they will be asked to do later as part of formal and summative assessment through examination.

The revised lesson supports progress that is more precisely framed than the learning envisaged in Martine's initial objectives. If we take the format Martine has used for her own objectives, we might arrive at these new expressions of intended learning:

- To recognise that readers' access to imagery is mediated by the point of view presented in the poem and that this shifts stanza by stanza across the poem.
- To understand the development of imagery relative to the notion of 'sight' and bearing witness.
- To understand the link between bearing witness and the poem's title.
- To express in writing the distinctive uses of imagery, the development in relation to point of view and the connection between these and the poem's title.

Tacit in each of these are the assumptions of Martine's initial objectives, but these revised objectives can only apply in this precision to *Dulce Et Decorum Est*. They cannot be transposed directly to another poem because they respond to the unique challenges of this one. These new objectives also suggest that sometimes the language a teacher uses to shape objectives pinpointing what they want pupils to learn may not be accessible for pupils in quite the same form. If we wanted to alter these for pupils we might frame them as questions:

- What imagery does Owen present to us?
- Through whose eyes/sight do we see this imagery?
- How is seeing in this way connected with the poem's title and its last four lines?

The final objective can be as simple as 'write a paragraph which answers these questions'.

Conclusion: applying this approach to other poems

This chapter began with a brief aside about *A Working Party* by Siegfried Sassoon. The objectives just applied to Owen's poem can't be applied directly to Sassoon's, nor any other poem, but the manner of thought can. We identified the role of nouns and verbs in a couple of extracts. If you look at the opening two stanzas of the poem you will see that further consideration along those lines could support conceptualised treatment. The first stanza has a preoccupation with movement, evident in the choice of verbs, and again some interest in diminished sight, compensated a little by the soldier's sense of sound. The portrayal of the soldier does not use figurative language, nor does it manipulate any single word class consistently, though there are a couple of telling adjectives. It could be that the dearth of vivid imagery is what is interesting here, especially relative to the other five stanzas, and so the approach to a lesson on Sassoon's poem might take account of the varying concentration of imagery in the poem across its entire structure. Once again, it would not suffice to make imagery the sole focus for pupils: if one did that for Owen's poem and again for this, pupils would not make progress other than in the texts covered. If they are to be equipped with ever more subtle skills, the core focus of imagery needs to be allied to something else, something unique to each study poem. Have a look at *A Working Party* in its entirety and consider how to mark its difference, and how that might be realised too in your guidance for pupils' writing.

Of course, if this way of approaching teaching poetry is to work, it has to apply to poetry other than that of the First World War. You can take a similar orientation to this poem by Thomas Hardy, called *Nobody Comes*:

> Tree-leaves labour up and down,
> And through them the fainting light
> Succumbs to the crawl of night.
> Outside in the road the telegraph wire
> To the town from the darkening land
> Intones to travelers like a spectral lyre
> Swept by a spectral hand.
>
> A car comes up, with lamps full-glare,
> That flash upon a tree:
> It has nothing to do with me,
> And whangs along in a world of its own,
> Leaving a blacker air;
> And mute by the gate I stand again alone,
> And nobody pulls up there.
>
> *– 9 October 1924*

Trust your own initial reading of the poem and build your approach from whatever strikes you and interests you at that point. Generate a line of questioning from there. You may be interested in the combination of the natural and man-made, and the poet/persona's apparent detachment from his surroundings. In terms of style, the second sentence is striking in its length and numerous 'l' sounds (are they intended to suggest the strings of the lyre, played one by one?). What would be the effect of guiding pupil response by putting them in the position of the persona, taking his perspective at the gate, and developing an activity for them to say what he sees, what he hears and what he feels?

I would choose to direct pupils to specific lines in order to support their hypotheses. From there it is possible to decide whether the information is overt or tacit. I might even plan to prompt questioning around a key detail. The idea of the telephone wires forming a 'spectral lyre' might serve this purpose. It can then act as a focus for pupils' thinking about how the persona perceives the world. What for him is the status of the 'spectral lyre' relative to reality or the imagination? What does it suggest of his view of the world, of fate, destiny, perhaps his weary resignation to greater forces?

The details you emphasise from one poem to the next will vary but the underlying approach of identifying aspects that can provide a key to understanding and deeper response holds true across many. This sort of preparation requires your judgement, and your careful balancing of the generic knowledge you have of form, of the writer's craft and of analysis with the elements that make the immediate poem for study unique and deserving of attention in the first place. When the balance is right, you will find that your lessons are far more than just 'poetry lessons'. Each experience will be unique because you have done justice to what each poem communicates, going some way to capture its unique response to the world.

References

Fenton, James (2002) *An Introduction to English Poetry*. London: Penguin/Viking.

Guppy, Pete and Hughes, Margaret (1999) *The Development of Independent Reading: Reading Support Explained*. Buckingham: Open University Press.

Hudson, Edward (1988) *Poetry of the First World War*. Hove: Wayland.

Hughes, Ted. (1967) *Poetry in the Making*. London: Faber.

Marshall, Bethan (2004) *English Assessed*. Sheffield: NATE.

Marshall, Bethan and Wiliam, Dylan (1990) *English Inside the Black Box*. London: Letts.

Meek, Margaret (1987) *How Texts Teach What Readers Learn*. Stroud: Thimble Press.

Padel, Ruth (2002) *52 Ways of Looking at a Poem, or How Reading Poetry Can Change Your Life*. London: Chatto & Windus.

CHAPTER 12

YOUR GROWTH AS AN ENGLISH TEACHER

Objectives of this chapter:

- To explain the requirements for schools as they support your early career development through induction
- To recognise growth as a teacher as a process of developing an ethos, and of developing the skills and knowledge to realise that ethos in practice
- To highlight the role of continued reflection as a foundation for your growth as a teacher of English
- To suggest means and resources to support your independent development as a teacher of English

---

Introduction

Induction can begin when you have successfully achieved qualified teacher status (QTS) and usually spans your first three terms of employment as a newly qualified teacher. Most new entrants to the profession complete these consecutively on a full-time basis across the first year of employment. In cases of part-time employment it can take longer, though the total period of induction will be equivalent. For example, if your first post is on a part-time 0.5 contract, your induction period will span two years. There are some exceptions. You are not legally obliged to complete an induction period if you intend to work only in the independent sector. The official guidelines include academies and free schools in this definition, as well as institutions of further education. Nevertheless, many institutions falling into this category will still opt to use some form of induction framework, and may opt in to the statutory requirements applicable to other schools.

Your induction period should be structured to develop the skills and knowledge you established during your course of initial teacher preparation. The aim of induction is to assist you in meeting the Teachers' Standards in your new context, sustaining the quality of your teaching consistently over the lengthier period of employment and with the additional demands of a first teaching post. Induction therefore continues assessment of your practice against the standards, just like your training programme. In addition, your school of first employment should provide a programme of professional development and support personalised to take account of your training needs. At each point in the process you can expect to be given guidance that assists you in developing and refining your teaching, often linked to specific standards.

Where the induction period spans a year, you will have an assessment at the end of each term. This is likely to be conducted by either your induction tutor or the head teacher. After the initial assessment, the head teacher reports to either the local authority or lead school in the local network, submitting details of your progress. After a third assessment in the third term, your head teacher will contact the same authority to make a recommendation regarding your progress against the standards and whether or not it has been satisfactory. The overarching authority then makes a final decision as to your successful completion of induction. It writes to both the National College for Teaching and Leadership and your head teacher to signal its decision. Finally the National College of Teaching and Leadership writes to you confirming the outcome. Hopefully you found that feedback throughout your induction was clear so that you anticipate the outcome at this point. Furthermore, hopefully the communication confirms your successful completion of induction and the full award of qualified teacher status.

What does the programme of support look like?

One aspect of the induction period that newly qualified teachers find very welcome is the slight reduction in teaching commitments. Your allocation of classes is still likely to increase on what you were used to during training, but you'll still find that you have a reduction so that your contact time will be 10 per cent less than that of your more experienced colleagues. You also have a statutory entitlement to a further 10 per cent of time reserved for planning, preparation and assessment activity, commonly referred to as PPA (planning, preparation and assessment) time. All teachers have this entitlement.

A key factor in your progress will be the input and support of your induction tutor. An experienced member of the school staff will take the role, though unlike the role of mentor during your training this may not be someone with a specialism in English. It is possible that one member of staff holds the induction tutor role and guides newly qualified teachers in several subjects across the school, and possibly across a network of schools. They will provide feedback for you on your teaching and professional work, though this is unlikely to match the frequency of feedback you experienced during training. Though there will be 'regular reviews of your progress' these may not be every week. However, you can expect to have a formal discussion with your tutor at the end of each term. You can also expect that from time to time, though again not weekly, your induction tutor will observe you teach and find opportunity to discuss your lesson afterwards. The tutor should provide regular written reviews of progress which will have both summative and formative purposes. You will also have continuing opportunity to observe the teaching of experienced and effective teachers to support your own development.

When colleagues review your progress, the comments should be linked to evidence and make reference to the standards. The induction tutor will provide objectives for your development relative to these and personalised to your own needs. You are expected to record evidence of your progress around these objectives and consistent with the steps agreed with your tutor.

The head teacher of your first post school has obligations too. Simply put, they must ensure that your duties and the conditions in which you work 'facilitate a fair and effective assessment of the newly qualified teacher's conduct and efficiency as a teacher against the relevant standards' (DfE, 2013: 12). There are a number of requirements a head teacher must address in addition to ensuring that your timetable is reduced and that you have the support of an induction tutor. Guidelines stipulate that they must 'not make unreasonable demands', must not 'normally demand teaching outside the age range and/or subject' for which you are employed to teach and must not present you, 'on a day-to-day basis, with discipline problems that are unreasonably demanding for the setting'. There are further details that suggest you should teach a range of classes, and that you will be involved in planning, teaching and assessment activity comparable to other teachers working in similar posts in the school. If you are asked to take on 'additional non-teaching responsibilities', you should be given support and have the necessary preparation.

When your induction tutor or head teacher complete their assessment of your practice, they will do so in response to these prompts drawn from the assessment record. They must describe:

- strengths;
- areas for further development where progress is satisfactory and areas of concern;
- evidence used to inform the judgements; and
- where appropriate, targets to be met.

They are asked to make reference to each of the eight Teachers' Standards. In turn, you are invited to comment on your experience of induction up to this point. You can comment on the extent to which you feel the report reflects training discussions you've had over the induction period and whether or not the support has met regulations and guidance. Most importantly for your growth as a teacher, you are asked to signal areas for development in the next stages of your career.

Continuity between your initial training and your induction year

The basic principle of ensuring some continuity between your initial programme of training and your first year of employment as a qualified teacher is long established. In recent years, the most visible means of ensuring the transfer of information was a document called the Career Entry and Development Profile (CEDP). This was completed by student teachers in the final stages of their training courses and required the contribution of their tutors to identify the main points for early professional development during induction. The mechanism had statutory status for the last time in 2012. However, the provision of reliable and useful information about a beginning teacher's strengths and development needs remains important. Many courses of teacher preparation continue to use a document like the CEDP, which seems sensible when the induction review documents already described in this chapter continue to express progress against the same set of Teachers' Standards.

Though the statutory requirement to complete a CEDP-style document has been relaxed, the responsibilities of all parties involved in transition and induction have increased and are scrutinised with more rigour. In summer 2014 the new framework for the inspection of teacher preparation programmes (Ofsted, 2014) for the first time embedded issues of transition in its procedural design. In the years up to 2014, Ofsted inspections of these courses were completed in a single visit, and could take place at any point in the training programme. Now inspections are in a two-stage format. In the first stage, an inspection team will assess a course in its final stage. The emphases include attention to the quality of students' teaching as they move towards meeting the Teachers' Standards, and encompass the accuracy of the training provider's own assessments of their attainment. The new feature is the second stage, in which an inspection team will observe a sample of newly qualified teachers in the first weeks of their induction post. This is intended as a means of gauging the quality of their training in preparing them for the demands of their early employment, and of further examining the accuracy of provider judgements about students' attainment of the Teachers' Standards. Clearly the role of the appointing school in early induction support may have some bearing on the confidence of a newly qualified teacher and their capacity to translate the strengths of their training into their early teaching. This revised inspection framework addresses the accountability of each party in this transition more comprehensively than ever before.

What do these circumstances mean for you if you are a beginning teacher of English, coming to the end of your training and anticipating the induction year ahead?

The prospect of an Ofsted inspector visiting your classroom so early in your work may sound daunting, though do keep in mind that the inspection is concerned with assessing the quality of training and support you have received rather than on making a judgement about your own performance. In practice, only a small number of beginning teachers qualifying from a particular course will experience this form of observation.

While the inspection process, especially the observation component, will be prominent if it happens to you, other aspects of the transition will be far more important in ensuring you feel secure and confident in your new role. You should feel you are able to develop your teaching swiftly, and it is likely that what happens in these early stages of employment also lays a foundation for your later career. The quality of information that passes between your training programme and your new school will be key to ensuring opportunities for such development are recognised and taken.

How do you grow as a teacher?

One newly qualified teacher of English, Ben, describes his experience of his first term in a paid post like this:

> My first experience of teaching wasn't just [me] and the students. There is a huge jumble of factors that come together to make up the work – it's government policy influences, it's your local authority, influences from your head teacher and your head of department and suddenly there's lots of paper coming in – 'this is what you have to do' – 'this is how much progress you have to make'. It hasn't disillusioned why I love teaching, but it is something that I put up with. So my opinions did change [as to what English teaching is]. It was all the wonderful things I thought it was but there were gremlins in that world that I hadn't thought about. (MacIntyre and Jones, 2014: 35)

His remarks express the impact of factors that are relevant to the experience of training to teach too but which are rarely at the heart of things so early on. Understandably, developing competence in the classroom is the main priority during training, even though the Teachers' Standards also require you to demonstrate appropriate professional conduct and some engagement with related issues. When Ben comments on the expectations placed upon him in terms of 'the progress you have to make', he highlights one major difference in his new capacity. He, like any newly qualified teacher, takes a position of direct responsibility – and hence accountability – for the progress of his pupils. While a commitment to pupil learning is to be expected of anyone working through a course of teacher preparation, the direct responsibility ultimately resides with other colleagues, often the usual teacher for each of the classes you guide during placement training. Ben finds that as he gains those same responsibilities himself as a newly qualified teacher, he is faced with further different tasks and different forms of engagement with various colleagues. He also signals his increased awareness of numerous institutional influences on his day-to-day work.

Though Ben describes these new demands on his energy as 'gremlins', his view of them as a little pernicious may change over time. You will get to know similar frameworks and get used to working in them. The better you know them, the easier it becomes to see how your own ethos can be realised within that context, and you will probably become more confident too in articulating your own perspective when you find a conflict of values or approach. Another student commenting in the same study remarked:

> It is only later with my own experiences and my own confidence to be the teacher that I want to be that I've felt that I can stand and say I actually don't agree. This is what I want the scheme of work to look like ... I am going to do it my way. But I couldn't do that at first. (McIntyre and Jones, 2014: 34)

This notion of being 'the teacher that I want to be' is an interesting one, suggesting subjective conceptions of the role are important alongside official conceptions of the role of teacher (currently outlined as a set of skills and competences in the Teachers' Standards) and relative to the terms and conditions of your employment. The clearest expression of these codified versions will likely be found in a job specification, often supplied on application for a post, and in your contract for employment. The subjective conceptions may be less easy to express, or at least to do so concisely, as they will be shaped by your own values and your own views about the purposes of English, what should comprise its content, and by your perspective on how young people learn the knowledge, skills and understanding you believe to be core to the discipline.

Considering these matters takes us full circle, echoing some of the interests of this book's first chapter about the knowledge of English teachers. At least some of the knowledge needed of teachers of English is dynamic. It has to change as communication and technologies in the wider world change. Where some of a teacher's knowledge is based on an understanding of curricular and assessment frameworks, that too will need updating every time those structures are altered. A good deal of development as a teacher will link with your capacity to keep pace with these changes and from the experience of working in the context of different systems over time.

Growth, though, is more than keeping up to date. It entails sustaining a reflective habit, an orientation to your role claimed by Tsui (2005) as an essential trait of the expert teacher. A case study by Turvey and Lloyd (2014) shows this sort of orientation in practice, describing the thought a beginning teacher, Jeremy, applies to his pupils' responses to *Great Expectations*. Jeremy shapes his approach around a question posed by Jerome Bruner:

What gives great fiction its power: what in the text and what in the reader? (Bruner, 1966: 4)

Jeremy argues that though the professional frameworks he works within frequently place importance upon the qualities of texts, the role of readers is less easily accommodated. He questions the usefulness of positing learning objectives for all pupils at the start of every lesson, and challenges the dominant preoccupation with pace as evidence of progress in learning. He believes these distract him, and teachers of English more generally, from paying heed to what pupils say or have to say about the texts they study. He feels this means lessons tend to follow a set agenda, working towards set outcomes, with little scope for responding to the interests of pupils or their entry points of engagement. His discussion invites teachers of English to reflect closely on the reactions pupils give as a means to inform their own teaching repertoires. Jeremy's experiences lead him to see there is no single correct model of teaching English. He is open to variety, to numerous possibilities. Elsewhere, Jones and McIntyre (2014: 29–30) cite Pike's acknowledgement (2011) of 'the significance to teachers of English of ethical professional and personal identities' and the way their subject knowledge and subject pedagogy combine as a basis for creating classrooms which are 'reflective and responsive' sites of learning. In Jeremy's case, because he is alert to the detail of what pupils do and its implications, his growth as a teacher derives from his own sensitive and empathetic approach.

Another way in which you can grow as a teacher is through the relationships you build with your colleagues and the extent to which your induction department creates a culture for development. Viv Ellis (2007) has explored subject knowledge development as something more than an individual enterprise, a process other than desk study alone, but one of engagement in department cultures. He sees all participants, beginning teachers included, as agents who negotiate interpretations of their role, of the discipline and of statutory obligations to create something unique, the character of the department arising from a fine balance of design, consensus, compromise and pragmatism. To some extent your early development as a teacher will involve making sense of the established department culture, but it could also be that you act to alter or improve the culture in some way. Many departments hope that newly qualified teachers join them with fresh ideas and original approaches, and actively invite you to contribute in such ways. At a very simple level, it may be that you have completed an English-based project or assignment during your training, and that you can bring findings or insights that are thought-provoking and useful for the department. From your point of view it can be fascinating how colleagues interpret or transform these and apply them in their own work.

One of the most useful activities you can continue, without incurring great expense to your school, is observation of other colleagues teaching. Inevitably your own experiences of teaching during initial training will not have required you to take responsibility for every single strand of the curriculum or every unit of assessment at GCSE. Schools rarely allocate classes in their last year of GCSE courses to student teachers. Contact with A-level classes can be equally slight, especially with groups approaching examinations. It is likely, though, that in your induction year you may teach a class in the final year of a course and preparing for high-stakes public examination.

On commencing your employment it is sensible to make clear to your induction tutor the extent of your experience in this respect, so that support for you can be planned. Your training provider may ask that you complete a document similar to the Career Entry and Development Profile. Whatever format you are asked to use, a signal about your experience with examination groups is also wise here. You could even indicate that you welcome the opportunity to shadow or observe more experienced colleagues as they teach classes getting ready for examination. Revision lessons and the teaching strategies to make them effective are often very different from lessons earlier in an academic year. They need to consolidate understanding, support pupils' capacity to recall salient detail, and give an opportunity for them to practise and refine techniques likely to support success in examination. Observation gives you an insight to relevant approaches and will also help you work in a style that is consistent with that of your team and the school. From the point of view of pupils this is also important. A consistent approach helps them transfer their revision skills across subjects, and is therefore likely to help them feel confident and well-prepared for examination.

Depending on the nature of your initial training, you may maintain contacts with peers who also have employment in the locality of your own school. Peer-observation with a trusted colleague from another institution can also be a useful catalyst for development. Where the activity is reciprocal, a visit elsewhere also gives you opportunity to see how things operate in a different department and can lead you to think afresh about the ethos and systems of your own team.

Leisure as professional growth

Because English involves communication and attention to texts of many types, almost all the situations you encounter and the texts you read in daily life have potential for use in the classroom. This can be both a joy and a burden, and often each concurrently. You may find yourself reading a novel that you have chosen entirely for pleasure, only to find that you stumble across a paragraph that you know will provide an excellent passage by which to explore the reliability of narrators. Junk mail through your door may not have any immediate use to you personally, but could be the basis of a lesson on persuasive language. Watching television or viewing online, you find that a post-match football interview offers excellent material for discourse analysis. The serendipity of finding teaching material like this can be a great pleasure, but it can also mean that it is hard to switch off and step away from a teacherly perspective. These things aside, the demands professional tasks of planning and assessment make on your time, and classroom teaching makes on your energy, make it a challenge to sustain your leisure interests in the way you did before teaching.

When you do read for pleasure, try to follow your interests and pursue reading for its own sake, as well as reading what you need to as a direct result of your professional role. In terms of your role of teacher, such reading might not have any immediate impact on your teaching. In the long term, however, it ensures your continuing enthusiasm for reading and your liveliness. It will allow you to make spontaneous asides about stories, characters, favourite lines and details whenever the opportunity arises, and to signal to pupils that you are not 'just' a teacher but someone who values reading regardless. Many student teachers joining the profession shortly after completion of their first degrees report the detrimental impact reading for obligation has had on them throughout their degree and successive examinations at GCSE and A-level. The same can happen while teaching when you will have to read certain texts according to examination specifications and the requirements of departmental schemes of work. Even practical factors can dictate what you work with, down to what stock is available in the department cupboard. Reading for yourself and without a work-based agenda can support your long-term effectiveness as a teacher and ultimately your enjoyment of the job.

Formal training

The organisations offering formal professional development training are many and diverse. Most specialists in the subject are aware of the National Association of Teachers of English (NATE), which offers training events, seminar discussion groups and its own annual conference.

The English and Media Centre (EMC) also provides training, often with sessions tailored to very specific units of GCSE and A-level courses, or to strands of the Key Stage 3 curriculum. These offer an independent alternative to the training sessions and briefings provided by examination boards themselves. Each form of training is very useful. As you might expect, the latter will be more closely geared to the minutiae of each board's specification, while the EMC sessions attend to more generalisable principles.

Both NATE and the EMC have remits that respond to the full English curriculum and the breadth of an English teacher's work. There are other agencies that specialise in areas relevant to the English curriculum, also offering resources and training. In relation to media, both Film Education and the British Film Institute (BFI) are helpful sources of guidance. Each offers material that continues to be relevant even where the National Curriculum has diminished the place of film, for instance in their resources concerning film adaptations of literary texts. The British Film Institute runs Master's-level courses, one-off education events and an annual conference. The Film Education website lists their many training events. The two also complement the work of the Media Education Association.

Most university departments offering teacher education courses (whether PGCE or School Direct) also offer further research in education, to masters and doctoral level. Academic staff in those institutions will have specialist interests in many different aspects of education, and frequently they too will organise conferences or seminars considering these. While these may not always be framed as professional training tailored for teachers, they provide thought-provoking content and an opportunity to meet with the many people involved in education through different roles and in different communities. In other cases, events are devised specifically with teachers in mind, either within local partnerships (e.g. involving all the schools offering placements for a PGCE programme), around a subject specialism, or drawing together students or colleagues connected by a virtual network for occasional workshops or study schools. Whether or not you completed your training in one of the universities close to your first appointment school, you should find any higher education department involved in teacher preparation also has strong links with the local teaching community. In some areas, such departments collaborate very closely with schools to provide structured training for your induction period and also around mentoring practice for your experienced colleagues. School networks can also fulfil a similar function, either distributing training specialisms across the network according to local expertise or convening training in a lead school for all associated members.

Online guidance

Most beginning teachers find the online support networks available to them absolutely invaluable. The Times Educational Supplement (TES) website has subject-based groups, and of course NATE has its own social networks. Edmodo is an educational variant of Facebook and therefore a perfect resource for any teacher wishing to network professionally without having to accept the wider profile that Facebook can bring. Many English teachers are active users of Twitter, sharing ideas or recommending materials for use. Given the medium, available guidance changes rapidly as do the items that might be regarded as 'must-reads' or those with most influence. It is a good idea to start at the NATE or TES sites and work from the recommendations you find there.

Conclusion

To some extent your growth as a teacher of English is inevitable providing you sustain a reflective approach to your work and maintain dialogue with both your local and national peers, whether through face-to-face conversation or online exchanges. Nevertheless, you will recognise areas of knowledge to develop as official requirements change but also as you develop your own depth and understanding of the help pupils need and the impact of different approaches. Even where you work with the same materials and use the same teaching sequence with different groups, you will often find differing outcomes. This could point to the limited value of generalisation in teaching – things are rarely the same twice. On the other hand, many of the means to develop as a teacher described above present or mediate research in English education. Research tends to seek findings that can be generalisable, that can be applied to different situations or which may be true of varying contexts. Your growth will often be a matter of improving your teacherly judgement, often balancing the underlying principles or research-informed strategies with the wisdom that derives from your own first-hand experience. I hope you find your development as a teacher of English is a long and happy process.

Websites

British Film Institute: http://www.bfi.org.uk
English and Media Centre: http://www.englishandmedia.co.uk

Film Education: http://www.filmeducation.org
Media Education Association: http://www.themea.org.uk
National Association of Teachers of English: http://www.nate.org.uk
Times Educational Supplement: http://www.tes.co.ukg221

References

Bruner, Jerome S. (1966) *Toward a Theory of Instruction*. Cambridge, MA: Belknap Press of Harvard University.

DfE (2013) *Statutory Guidance on Induction for Newly Qualified Teachers (England)*. Reference: DFE-00090-2013.

Ellis, Viv (2007) 'Taking subject knowledge seriously: from professional knowledge recipes to complex conceptualizations of teacher development', *Curriculum Journal*, 18 (4): 447–62.

McIntyre, Joanna and Jones, Susan (2014) 'Possibility in impossibility? Working with beginning teachers of English in times of change', *English in Education*, 48 (1): 26–40.

Ofsted (2014) *Initial Teacher Education Inspection Handbook*. Reference: 140094.

Pike (2011) 'Developing as an ethical English teacher: valuing the personal and poetic in professional learning', *English in Education*, 45 (3): 224–36.

Tsui, Amy B. M. (2005) 'Expertise in teaching: perspectives and issues', in K. Johnson (ed.), *Expertise in Second Language Learning and Teaching*. Basingstoke: Palgrave Macmillan, pp. 167–89.

Turvey, Anne and Lloyd, Jeremy (2014) 'Great Expectations and the complexities of teacher development', *English in Education*, 48 (1): 76–92.

INDEX

abridgement of script 132–5, 141, 143
academia 13
academy schools 17
accent 12, 33, 42
adaptation, of novels to plays 38; of novels to
    films 133, 184
adjacency pairs 78, 81, 83, 84
adjectives 45–53, 66–8, 90, 144, 150–1, 161–2,
    165, 172
adolescence 7
adverbials, fronted 90
adverbs, 47, 48, 53, 68, 90, 144, 161
advertisements 103–10, 113–15
advertising 107, 109, 110, 112–13
affective dimension, demands of texts 42, 54;
    response 60, 152
affective response 42, 54, 60, 152
affordance 48, 69, 146, 156
AFOREST (acronym) 120–1
A Language for Life 74
A Swift Pure Cry 68
A Working Party 161, 165
A-level 43, 65, 182–4; English Language 5;
    English Literature 82, 132, 154, 161;
    Theatre Studies 5
alliteration 58, 106, 120

Almond, David 68–71
aloud, reading 36, 40, 63, 80
analogy 17, 54
analysis, of language chapter 4, 108,
    113, 115, 183; of literature 37,
    chapter 3, 60, 63–5, 135–41, 150–9,
    165–7, 173
annotation 25, 77, 78, 80, 83, 148, 158
appearance 37, 48, 50–1, 136–8
apostrophe 87, 93–9
appropriacy 90
argument 94, 98–9, 110, 119, 122, 123, 126;
    counter-argument 98
assessment 9, 12, 14, 17, 25, 26, 40, 41, 47,
    84, 87, 88, 91, 96, 99, 115, 118, 119, 120,
    121, 129, 164, 183; criteria 121, 122, 123,
    128; formative, framework 18, 22, 125,
    180; GCSE 75, 182; of NQT teacher 175–8;
    peer- 61, 63, 70, 124, 126, 170; self- 124,
    170; summative 171
assessment for learning 58, 59, 122, 124
assessment levels 18
audience 19, 60, 114, 119, 121, 125, 126, 131,
    135–9, 141–3, 145, 147, 156–9; response of
    109, 122, 151, 154; target 103–9, 114
audio-visual texts 79, 84, 101, 106

author 44, 47, 51, 55, 58, 70, 102, 103, 157;
    author's craft 45, 52, 60, 67; pupils as 61,
    63, 64, 80

band descriptors 124–5
Barker, Ronnie 158
Barnes, Douglas 74
basic interpersonal communication skills
    (BICS) 83
Bergson, Henri 155–7
Bernstein, Basil, elaborated code 61
BFI, British Film Institute 184
Black, Paul and Wiliam, Dylan 124
Boal, Augusto 141
Boots the Chemists 87
Branagh, Kenneth 133, 140, 142
Britton, James 45, 74
Bruner, Jerome 24, 180

CALPS (Cognitive Academic Language
    Proficiency) 83
camera shot 115
canon, canonical texts 4, 60, 65, 103, 112–13
careers advice 110
Carnegie Medal award 65
causality 21
CEDP 177, 178
chain of schools 17
Chaplin, Charlie 156
character 3, 16–23, 33–55, 66, 69, 105,
    chapter 9, chapter 10, 161, 165, 181, 183
characterisation 7, 21, 22, 45
Children Go Online 112
citizenship 110
civic culture, 112
CivicWeb 112, 114
class (social) 147, 148, 158
class novel 33
classifying, classification 7, 52–5, 144, 156,
    161, 165
classroom management 2, 33, 75
Cleese, John 158
climax 134–6
cloze exercise 25
cognitive domain 62
colleagues 7–9, 11, 29, 176, 179, 181–4
comedy 154–8
comic relief 154
community 7, 8, 110, 129, 184
complex sentences 3, 87
composition 59–61, 92–3
comprehension 6, 20, 38, 40, 42, 48, 50, 79,
    133, 138, 143, 152

concept formation 128
continuum 127, 151
Conversation Analysis 82
Corbett, Ronnie 158
couplet 164
creative writing 2, 57
criteria, assessment 91, 118, 121–5, 128
critical literacy 103, 110, 114
cues 36, 38, 62, 138, 149, 153, 158
culture 111; civic 112, department 181; high
    and low 157; local 112; popular 129;
    pupils' 4; subject 8
curriculum reform 18, 87

Dead Poets' Society 32
debating 119, 146
decoding 37, 89
deixis 97
demarcation 90
department, English 4, 8, 17–19, 40, 43, 129,
    154, 162, 179, 181, 183; university 184
Department for Education 87, 90
design, choices in writing 45, 93, 98; of lessons
    chapter 1, 60, 75, 76, 86, 96, 103, 104,
    118, 128, 131, 133, 160; of curriculum
    74, 111, 112; of resources 98; of task 114,
    141, 153
Dewey, John 7, 8
diagnostic device 11, 28, 29
dialect 12, 42, 54
dialogic talk 129
dialogue 3, 8, 22, 23, 25, 33, 38, 42, 53, 5, 64,
    65, 97, 113, 128, 133, 140, 141, 146, 147,
    152, 153, 185
Dickens, Charles 45, 49, 51, 154
differentiation 26, 120, 143
directors 141, 158
Discourse Analysis 82, 183
discourse, academic 79, 83
Dowd, Siobhan 68, 69
drama chapter 10, 5, 21, 83, 102, 131,
    135, 141
dramatic effects 131
Dulce et Decorum est 160–71

EAL (English as an Additional Language) 83
Edmodo 185
Educating Rita 147, 150, 157–8
effectiveness, of teaching 11, 48, 92,
    183; of texts chapter 4, 94, 110, 122,
    123, 128
elaborated code 61
Ellis, Viv 8, 181

EMC (English and Media Centre) 75, 184
emotion 21, 33, 42, 58, 60, 62, 67, 103, 122, 127, 134–6, 140–4, 146, 151–3, 167
emotive language 120
empathy 21, 37, 38, 48
encoding 89
enfranchisement 102, 112, 129
English language 5, 82
English Language (A-level) 74, 88, 89, 102
English Literature 5, 18, 89, 91
equilibrium 134–6
equivocal situation 157
ethos 7, 16, 43, 64, 82, 113, 174, 180, 182
exaggeration 156
examination questions 45, 60, 154
examinations, specifications 4, 8, 12, 18, 22, 42, 45, 60, 91, 120, 125, 128–9, 154, 164, 171, 183–4
expertise 2, 4, 8, 11, 21, 59, 120, 139, 180, 184

facts 120
Farrell, J.G. 154
feedback 24, 58, 59, 62, 77, 92, 93, 96, 107, 134–5; at induction 175, 176; observation 2, 3, 11, 36, 62, 164
figurative language 20, 22, 66, 68, 161, 172
film 26, 32, 48, 65, 79, 85, 106, 133, 140, 155, 156, 158, 162, 163, 167, 184
film adaptation 26, 133, 140, 158, 184
Film Education 184
first person 51, 54–5, 69, 168
first teaching post 112
First World War 114, 146, 162, 172
fluency 36–7, 39, 63, 74, 83, 119
Fones, Deborah 137
formal assignment 16
Forster, E.M. 148
forum theatre 141–2, 158
Framework for Secondary English 102
free schools 17, 175

Gagné 24, 26
GCSE 18, 22, 65, 74, 75, 89, 91, 120, 154, 160, 182–4
genitive tense 95, 97
genre 98, 99, 102, 119, 146, 156
gesture 33, 85, 135, 138, 140–2, 152
Gibson, Rex 131, 141
globalisation 111
glossary 81, 82, 109
Glossary of Terms 90

Gove, Michael 8, 42, 86, 87
government policy 179
grammar 4, 6, 12, 18, 20, 74, chapter 6, 102, 119
Grammar for Writing? 92, 98
grapheme 89
Great Expectations 45, 49, 51, 55, 180
ground rules 33, 157
group work 77, 106, 139, 142–3, 148
Gulliver's Travels 154

Hardy, Thomas 172
HAT (History of Advertising Trust) 113
head teachers, union of 89, role in induction 175–9
Heaven's Eyes 68–70
Henry V 131, 132, 141, 144
high-order thinking 53
Hobbes, Thomas 157
Holes 154
homophone 38, 91
humour chapter 10
hyperbole 99, 139

IBM 88
identities 74, 147, 181
imagination 3, 32, 47, 48, 51–4, 60, 141, 168, 173
impact of teaching 2, 19, 20, 30, 32, 39, 42, 76, 81, 85, 92, 96, 99, 164, 183, 185
imperatives 33, 106, 129
improvisation 146, 152–3
inclusion 38
induction, 39, chapter 12
inference 53, 143
instructional event 24
intelligent action 7
internet 103
intonation 80, 82, 141–2, 147
Investigating Spoken Language 75
irony 78, 103, 138, 139, 143, 156, 159

jargon 52, 83, 84, 156
job application 180
judgement, teacherly 1–3, 7, 12, 26, 39, 42, 59, 64, 76, 80, 85, 137, 147, 173, 185

Keaton, Buster 156
Kes 32
knowledge-in-action 2, 8
knowledge 18, 21–9, 47, 71, 84, 91–2, 102, 108–12, 115, 125, 152, 157, 161, 173, 174–5, 180–1, 185

labelling 92, 96, 161
Labour 87, 102
language analysis chapter 5
language development 128
language resource 47, 49, 51, 54, 55
Laughter 155
learning objectives chapter 1, 18–29, 44, 46–7, 60, 64, 77, 78, 82, 93, 97, 103, 115, 137, 163, 166, 181
Leda and the Swan 167
Lee, Rebecca 86–8
lesson planning and design chapter 1
library 7, 65
linguistics 5, 59, 73, 74, 80, 81, 84, 91, 95, 102, 110, 113, 119, 128
Literacy Progress Units 96
literacy, standards 88
literary models chapter 4; literary analysis chapter 3; literary jargon 52; literary reading chapter 2, chapter 3, chapter 9, chapter 10, chapter 11; literary texts chapter 3
literature, study of 2, 7, 16, 21, 26, 40, 73, 78, 83, 91, 102, 112, 113, 115, 119, 134, 135, 184
Lloyd, Harold 156
location 37, 51, 69, 97
London School, the 74

Macbeth 34–5, 38, 167
magazines 103, 106, 113–15
malapropism 158
Margaret Meek 46–7
media education chapter 7
Media Education Association 184
media literacy programme 112
Media Studies 79
mentor mentoring 8, 9, 11, 17, 107, 150, 176, 185
metalanguage 82, 88, 111
metaphor 5, 48–50, 156, 168
mind's eye 52, 58, 165–8
misconceptions 12–13
mnemonic 120
mobile technology 108, 111
models, of English 4–6, of grammar 82, 94, literary chapter 4
modes of communication 22, 25, 79, 84, 103, 111, 113–15, 125, 129, 164
morphemes, morphology, morpho-syntactic awareness 95
Mortimer, Bob 156
motivation, of characters 20, 21, 148, 153–4; of pupils 24, 64

moving image texts 102–3, 112–15
multiliteracies chapter 7
music 17, 41, 106

narrative 32, 34, 37, 40–1, 53–4, 57–9, 64–5, 69–71, 98, 112, 136, 139
NATE (National Association of Teachers of English) 183
National College of School Leadership 175
national identity 74
National Literacy Strategy 12
network, of schools 175–6; virtual 184–5
New London Group 111
newspapers 92, 106, 108, 113–15
Nineteen-eighty-four 66, 68, 119
Nobody Comes 172
noun 47, 171; concrete 51, 53, 55, 161; plural 93; proper 68, 69
noun phrase 52, 161
NQT (Newly Qualified Teacher) chapter 12

Ofsted 110–11, 129, 178
online journalism 112
opening sentences 58, 66, 69
oral feedback 93
Oranges Are Not the Only Fruit 154
orthography 80–1
Orwell, George 65–7, 119
overlapping 80
Owen, Wilfred chapter 11

paralinguistic communication 80–1
parody 156
pastiche 156
pauses, in analysis of spoken language 82; in reading 31, 32, 34, 36, 37, 39, 46, 63, 64
peer-observation 182
personal response 108
persuasion 104–10, 115, 119–27
phonemes 89
phonics 89, 95
placement 9, 11, 12, 17, 29, 75, 148, 162, 179, 184
play script 38–9, 76, 78, 80, chapter 10
point-evidence-explain paragraphing 45–7, 134–9
popular culture 129
PowerPoint 16, 17, 26, 104, 163
précis 139
presentation, in texts 20, 44–5, 54, 62, 70, 115, 138, 145, 164; spoken language 119–27, 146–7, 156; teacher's 12, 13, 16–17, 22–6, 55, 79, 104

primary phase 86, 89, 96
print media 101
problem-solving 80, 84, 142
pronoun 96–7, 99, 106
protagonists 19, 66, 147
pseudo words 89
punctuation 34, 36, 64, 86–7, 89–91, 155
puns 106, 156, 158
purposes of texts 45, 60, 61, 93, 103–4, 108,
    115, 118–29, 136, 146

quotations 19, 23, 44–5, 53, 60, 115, 133–6,
    139, 152, 169–70
QTS (Qualified Teacher Status) 174

radio 113, 155
reading 4, 6, 8, 11, 16, 20, 22, chapter 2,
    chapter 3, chapter 4, 80, 89, 101, 102,
    110–15, 119, chapter 9, chapter 10,
    chapter 11, 183
recall, pupils' 24, 64, 78, 108, 138, 162, 182
Reeves, Vic 156
Removing the Barriers to Literacy 129
repertoire 25, 32, 36, 43, 54, 55, 59, 69, 124–5,
    143, 147, 164, 181
representation 32, 79, 54, 74, 89, 152
research evidence 86, 91–2
rhetorical questions 105–6, 120, 127,
    138–9
rhyme 166
Room 101 119–23, 129
rotation activity 106–8
Russell, Willy 147, 152, 156

sarcasm 158
satire 156
scaffolding 24, 56, 61, 69, 135
School Direct 184
Second World War 33
secondary phase 5, 74, 88, 89
sentence combining 92
sentence stems 127–8
sequence, for teaching 12, 16, 24–5, 29, 45–55,
    59, 60–4, 77, 80, 88, 120, 139, 165, 185;
    sequencing in text 70, 85, 97, 105, 140,
    149, 151–2, 156, 170
sestet 168
shared annotation 77
silences 82, 142
simile 48–50, 69, 163, 165, 168
Slaughterhouse 5 154
SLCN (Speech Language and Communication
    Needs) 129

slogan 106
social change 74
social context 34, 41, 114
social interaction 46, 128
social-constructivism 128
sociolinguistics 74
soliloquy 40, 159
sonnet 113
sound-letter correspondence 95
SpAG 91
speech 34, 38, 77, 78, 87, 115, 141, 142,
    150, 156
speeches chapter 8, 146
Spoken Language Study 74, 76
stagecraft chapter 9
Standard English 91–2, 125
stanza 39, 163–71
statistics 120
Stoppard, Tom 154
subordinate clause 66, 98
suffix 91
superiority theory 157–8
syntactic unit 82
syntax 92, 97
systematic review 92, 96

tag-line 105
television 65, 75, 76, 103, 105, 109, 113–15,
    119, 129, 155, 162, 183
television interview 75
tension 33, 39, 63, 88, 99, chapter 9,
    154, 159
The Boy in the Striped Pyjamas 33, 37, 42
The Class Sketch 158
The Importance of Being Earnest 154
The One Show 75, 82
The Siege of Krishnapur 154
The Wrong Mans 158
Thinkbox 109–10, 113–14
Thinking Together 129
Times Educational Supplement 185
Titus Andronicus 167
tone 33, 35, 63–4, 99, 139, 142–3, 148–53,
    158
topic sentences 123, 140
tragedy 154, 159
transcription chapter 5, 113
transcripts 113
transition, between schools 90; from training to
    first post 178
triplets, rhetorical 120
trope 156
Tsui, Amy 180

turns, conversational 78–82
Turvey and Lloyd 180
Twitter 185
two-hander 147, 156

values 6, 7, 13, 16, 43, 74, 109, 147,
    180, 183
viewing 77, 79, 81, 111, 156, 167, 183
viewing habits 109
viral campaigns 103
Visit Norfolk (website) 99
visual humour 156

vocabulary 4, 11, 20, 36–7, 66, 89–91, 102, 119,
    125–7, 135–40, 144, 151, 156, 158, 159,
    161; specialist chapter 5
voiceovers 113

writing 2, 4, 8, 11, 16, 22, 40–2, chapter 4, 84,
    89–94, 98–9, 102–3, 107, 111–13, 117,
    119–20, 123, 131, 134–6, 139–44, 146, 157,
    164, 168–72

Yeats, W.B. 167
Yes He Can 129